May you enjoy these summer sermons
Betty Shirley

Walking With Christ

Sermons For
The Summer Season

Michael D. Wuchter
submitted by Shirley Dyer Wuchter

Shirley Dyer Wuchter

CSS Publishing Company, Inc., Lima, Ohio

WALKING WITH CHRIST

Library of Congress Cataloging-in-Publication Data

Wuchter, Michael D.
  Walking with Christ : sermons for the summer season / Michael D. Wuchter.
    p. cm.
  ISBN 0-7880-2603-8 (perfect bound : alk. paper)
  1. Pentecost—Sermons. 2. Common lectionary (1992). 3. Sermons, American—20th
century. 4. Lutheran Church—Sermons. I. Title.

  BV61.W83 2009
  252'.041—dc22

                                                                    2008027838

For more information about CSS Publishing Company resources, visit our website at
www.csspub.com or email us at csr@csspub.com or call (800) 241-4056.

Cover design by Barbara Spencer
ISBN-13: 978-0-7880-2603-4
ISBN-10: 0-7880-2603-8   PRINTED IN USA

The twelve sermons in this volume complete a journey with Christ through the year. This collection walks through the summer season. This gathering is a labor of love by Shirley Dyer Wuchter drawn from her husband's preaching over thirty years in parishes in New Jersey, Minnesota, Wittenberg College, and Namibia — biblically haunting, life-applicable, facing fears, living forgiveness. I've read them while undergoing cancer treatment, grateful for the emphasis on life now, as well as to come.

John Reumann
Professor Emeritus
Lutheran Theological Seminary
Philadelphia

In this fourth book of sermons, Michael Wuchter gives us even more creative images to convey and carry the words of the gospel. On Earth Day, he imagines a creation bogged down by government regulations; he balances the dangers of prayer with the risks of a roller coaster ride; and he comes to terms with the true meaning of sin and grace while camping next to some unruly families from Brooklyn.

These twelve sermons are chock full of illustrations that bring God's word alive. You can almost smell the bread as he describes a bakery in Manhattan, and you can feel both the raw tension and emerging unity in the diverse communities of the Namibian Church. Wuchter gives us himself and his insights in these carefully crafted sermons. They are both a joy and a challenge to read.

Reverend John D. Morris
Prince of Peace Lutheran Church
Dublin, Ohio

Michael Wuchter was a master of the English language and an excellent, excellent preacher.

Jerry L. Schmalenberger
Former President, Pacific Lutheran
  Theological Seminary
Affiliated faculty, Lutheran Theological
  Seminary, Hong Kong
Affiliated faculty, Huri Kristen Batak Protesten
  Seminary, Sumatra

One cannot help but be deeply moved by these sermons. In them, themes such as humility, respect, servanthood, accountability, forgiveness, and care of the creation point to the proclamation that we are all formed by the Triune God; fashioned out of the same clay, we are all part of the human community. Michael Wuchter conveys this sense of grateful connectedness in keen observations of the stuff of daily life. Whether he describes the pleasures of gardening or muses thoughtfully while emptying an old billfold, this fine preacher invites us to find meaning and joy in being part of God's good creation.

Daniel F. Martensen, Ph.D.
Former Director
Department of Ecumenical Affairs, ELCA

Michael Wuchter reflects his creative writing and preaching skills by focusing on the familiar and contemporary experiences of his readers and integrating them into God's story as revealed in Jesus Christ. His vibrant preaching ministry over the years to congregational and university communities come alive in these messages.

Edwin L. Ehlers
Retired Bishop
New Jersey Lutheran Synod

I am writing to share my thoughts after reading the manuscript for the fourth book of sermons by the Reverend Doctor Michael D. Wuchter, published posthumously by his wife, Shirley. This book is a collection of summer sermons — from the Day of Pentecost in 1975 and continuing through the Pentecost season of 1999 — from the many sermons originally shared with various congregations over that span of 23+ years. My wife and I are longtime friends of Michael and Shirley's — classmates during our college days at Wittenberg University — and have supported and encouraged Shirley in the preparation of these writings following Michael's sudden death in the summer of 2000. I continue to support the preparation of Michael's sermons, and hopefully of some of his prayers in the future, because I am convinced that Michael's insights and the beauty and clarity of his messages of hope, of healing and reconciliation are necessary and valuable in today's world. Let me share with you what I find in this manuscript — beyond the words and ideas of a friend.

As I read his words — shared with so many over those two decades of preaching — I am often struck by the sense of rhythm within these sermons. From the repetition of Nicodemus' words "How can these things be true?" to the "in and out" description of zoom books, I appreciated the repetition and rhythms in the words and in the ideas. As I think about their meaning for me, I especially appreciate the feeling of continuity in creation and in God's continuing creative activity and in the reconciliation of our selves with this creation. In short, these sermons represent yet another opportunity for me to reflect on Michael's insightful description of these ordinary events and situations that point me to the extraordinary relationship I am offered in the life and words of Jesus Christ.

Thomas J. Evans
Assistant Director
Wisconsin Geological and
Natural History Survey

Michael Wuchter's writing is a delight. His shifting and many-faceted themes return again and again to the essentials of Christian faith for the individual, the community, and society. Wuchter preached with such detail and precision — how he much have held the attention of those who came to listen. He looks with honesty and candor at the fears, vanities, and injustices of our day and speaks to them with the springtime promise of God's love.

Ann E. Hafften
Writer and editor,
Weatherford, Texas

I laughed when the station wagons from Brooklyn invaded the quiet of the Wuchter campsite. I cried when the middle-aged victim of a childhood rape held on tight to her anger and hatred instead of finding freedom in forgiveness. My mouth watered and my heart was glad when I read about the uniting power and the wonderful magic of bread. It is one more visit with pastor, mentor, colleague, and friend, Michael Wuchter, who was taken from us too soon.

Pastor Carol Hertler
Chillicothe, Ohio

Acknowledgments

Had it not been for so many people walking with me in my grief journey after my husband's sudden death, and had it not been for so many prayer partners, I would not have been able to outdistance the grief. I would not have been able to begin to produce this book, the fourth in a series organized according to the church year.

In shedding layers of loss over the last eight years, I thank two groups that have continued to meet on a regular basis and fulfill my personal and writing needs: the Wednesday Morning Prayer Group at First Lutheran Church in Duluth, Minnesota, and the Lake Superior Writer's Memoir Group. Thanks also to the First Lutheran Church Writer's Group who add encouragement to my literary pursuits.

I thank God for my exceptionally loving family, immediate and extended, and my many friends, local and global. Instrumental in leading me to CSS Publishing Company were three colleagues of my husband's at Wittenberg University: Dr. William A. Kinnison, President Emeritus; Dr. E. Charles Chatfield Jr., Professor Emeritus, History; and Dr. Richard P. Veler, General Secretary Emeritus and Professor Emeritus, English.

Also thanks to clergy and parishioners, particularly in Duluth, who supported this vision. I am indebted to those who wrote recommendations: to local editor, Dave Benson, and to CSS Publishing Company's editor, Becky Allen, and her staff who facilitated the project.

Ultimately, all thanks go to God: *Soli Deo Gloria.*

Table Of Contents

Introduction

Although summer is the season of Michael's death, it is also the season of life, of good memories, and of a time when his sermons drew upon summer images — gardening, fishing, visiting Coney Island, and traveling to Namibia. It was on the second trip to Namibia, a mission trip, when he became dizzy and died suddenly of heart failure. Five years later, I was able to read his sermons with more joy than sorrow and to begin compiling his writings into books:

- *Uplifting Christ Through Autumn, Sermons For The Fall Season*, 2006
- *Shining Through The Darkness, Sermons For The Winter Season*, 2007
- *Growing In Christ, Sermons For The Spring Season*, 2008

The process has helped in the transforming journey of relating to my beloved, no longer my dearest companion on earth but still a kindred spirit and helpmate in a new and mysterious way.

In life, he was a devoted pastor, always striving to relate the gospel to our everyday lives. I like to think that in death, his ministry continues through reading his sermons and sharing them with others.

— Shirley Dyer Wuchter
May 2008
Duluth, Minnesota

The Day Of Pentecost/Mother's Day/Parents' Weekend
Genesis 11:1-9; Acts 2:1-21;
John 15:26-27; 16:4b-11

Gardens

Now the whole earth had one language and the same words. And as they migrated from the east, they came upon a plain in the land of Shinar and settled there.

The Lord came down to see the city and the tower, which mortals had built. And the Lord said, "Look, they are one people, and they have all one language; and this is only the beginning of what they will do; nothing that they propose to do will now be impossible for them. Come, let us go down, and confuse their language there, so that they will not understand one another's speech." So the Lord scattered them abroad from there over the face of all the earth, and they left off building the city. Therefore it was called Babel, because there the Lord confused the language of all the earth; and from there the Lord scattered them abroad over the face of all the earth.   — Genesis 11:1-2, 5-9

When the day of Pentecost had come, they were all together in one place. And suddenly from heaven there came a sound like the rush of a violent wind, and it filled the entire house where they were sitting. Divided tongues, as of fire, appeared among them, and a tongue rested on each of them. All of them were filled with the Holy Spirit and began to speak in other languages, and the Spirit gave them ability.   — Acts 2:1-4

When the Advocate comes, whom I will send to you from the Father, the Spirit of truth who comes from the Father, he will testify on my behalf. You also are to testify because you have been with me from the beginning.
                  — John 15:26-27

I have received my *Smith & Hawken Catalogue* for the summer. If I had the money, I could order a ratchet anvil pruner with such a powerful cutting action that it can sever branches up to three-quarters of an inch in diameter. Or I could order a shuffle hoe with an angled blade that cuts weeds just below the crown. I could order a Dutch hand-weeder that is indispensable for working borders, and I am so attracted to border lines — or a Scottish composting fork. Sometimes I think all the cycles and responsibilities of life are contained in a Smith & Hawken gardening catalogue.

It is a good time of year for the study of phenology, the science of appearances; it is a good time to study the cycles in biological events and how they respond to light and climate. For example, when forsythia was in bloom, gardeners knew it was the proper time to prune the rosebushes, which by then had green buds on their canes.

When new oak leaves are about the size of a squirrel's ear (or the ear of a field mouse — there has been some serious debate about this), then the soil is warm enough to plant corn or beans. If they are planted before this natural signal, the ground would be too cold and the seed would not germinate. (The Algonquin Indians knew that 1,000 years ago.)

Phenology is the science of appearances. I don't know about you, but there is something about Mother's Day and gardening. It's the right time to go out and dig in the earth, and plant some life there with hope for beauty and fruit and the future.

The science of appearances — I want to examine more than appearances on this Mother's Day, Parents' Weekend, and Day of Pentecost. I want to examine with you the topic of gardening and human relationships and the good news, especially on the Day of Pentecost.

We could consider transcultural truth and gardens, and how the pentecostal spirit calls us into universal unity, willing us to speak all the languages of the good earth.

At Princeton University, there is a professor of the history of architecture who believes adamantly that gardens should be treated with academic respect because they reveal cultural philosophies. The thesis is that different cultures developed different gardening patterns reflecting lifestyles, political structures, and even attitudes toward nature and God and hope.

In the sixteenth century, for example, formal French gardens were laid out by wealthy landowners with rigidity and symmetry in a subconscious attempt to prove that nature was under their domination, just as the French people were under the absolute power of the king and his friends who owned the formal gardens. During the same time period, formal Italian gardens, many maintained by cardinals of the Roman Catholic church, accepted the finitude of human power and the fact that plants both bloom and die. Flowers in their gardens were allowed to go to seed, but the French replaced flowers the minute they began to fade. In arrogance and idolatry, they wanted control over both life and death.

On the other hand, the gardens of Ming Dynasty scholars were tended in the hope of capturing the pure state of natural harmony beyond the chaos that often sweeps through our living together. In their gardens, the Ming scholars attempted to capture peace and harmony, the balance of flowing water and solid rock, the fragile flower and the eternal human spirit. They wanted to contain in their small backyards the kingdom of God. Here was a pentecostal hope for the unity of the divine promise.

What would this type of study say about our US culture today? According to a recent *New York Times* magazine article on trendsetting contemporary gardens, we are in an "American Garden Revolution." It is the age of the "new romantic garden," a garden for all seasons, marked by lush plantings of decorative grasses that blend with the landscape and can be viewed with interest all year long: ornamental grasses and shrubs and perennials with lasting meaning, not quick spring thrills, not just a splash of summer fun and color before facing the reality of cold winter death, but something that lasts, that stays around to comfort us, to center us. We want some lasting meaning and hope, open for some Holy Spirit.

But on this Pentecost and this Mother's Day, I believe it would be most appropriate not to attempt a cultural analysis in light of the mission of the whole church, but rather it is a good day to dig for something more personal. I want to spade down into the gardens of our own unique history and hope.

Karel Capek (1890-1938), the author of a book titled, *The Gardener's Year*, first published in 1929, is a connoisseur of earth. He wrote that when digging, the dirt should, "crumble, but not break into lumps ... it must not make slabs, or blocks, or honeycombs, or dumplings; but, when you turn it over with a full spade, it ought to breathe with pleasure and fall into a fine and puffy tilth."

I am for pleasure and fine sifting, but let us also be honest as we dig into our gardens, because it is not really humus we are digging in, but history.

If you really do garden and often dig in cultivated soil, you know this to be true; one often finds himself becoming an amateur archeologist. Garden soil consists primarily of special ingredients, such as leaf mould, peat, stones, pieces of glass, and old mugs, broken dishes, nails, wire, bones, arrowheads, silver paper from long-consumed chocolate bars, broken bricks, old coins, pipes, tins, bits of string, buttons, soles of shoes, dog droppings, coal, pot handles, washbasins, buckles, rusted horseshoes, insulating material, scraps of newspapers, and innumerable other components, which the astonished gardener digs up at every stirring of the beds.

Let's look first at some of this history into which we wish to plant our hopes. If we are honest, one thing we will all turn up is that old Tower of Babel story from the book of Genesis, the book of beginnings. It is a story that first appears from our present perspective to be so odd, so old, so alien, and so primitive, and yet it has a certain hypnotic character of recognition. "Once upon a time, all the world ..." it begins. You must be careful with stories that begin with "once upon a time" because that could be anytime! But as I study this story in my archeological dig of our individual gardens, it carries me back into the earthen layers of millennia, back into what I had assumed were past strata of time. Then there occurs, as often happens when one studies the Old Testament, a shock of realization, the realization that what I am actually digging into is my own time. We turn back the soil and uncover our own time. It is a probing into our human spirit.

When you brush aside the dirt, it becomes apparent that ancient Babel is our city, and that we walk through the ruins of the tower on our way to class or on our way to work; this is the land of Shinar.

"Once upon a time, all the world spoke a single language...." We are back into the misty, opening morning in the Garden of Eden. We are back to when the mind had just been set free to range beyond the search for good and warmth and shelter, to when our human mind was first asking, "Why?" What difference does it make how we treat each other? Upon a grassy plain in the land of Shinar, planting those first proto-gardens of tubers and grains and wondering why there is division between us as human beings, divided not by distance, but by some perceived difference, not by race really but by rage. Why separation? Why the otherness? Why the lack of human compassion and communication between us at times, even between mother and child, sister and brother, husband and wife, friend and neighbor? It should not be this way!

This is the land of Shinar. Never trust a story that begins, "Once upon a time."

Once upon a time, there was unity, one language. We communicated to one another clearly; we understood each other, each other's deepest feelings, and we accepted each other in that unity, that trust, that peace. There was a binding center to all meaningful futures together. Now and always this is God's will for us, alluding to the Christ of Pentecost; God sends the Holy Spirit to offer just this gift.

Then the human, once upon a time, in his and her freedom, your freedom and my freedom, said, "I know the purpose of things, and it is centered around me. Come, let us build ourselves a tower with its top in the heavens, and we can be God. Let us eat from the tree of knowledge in the center of the garden called Eden. No one else is in charge except me." But without God, with no ultimate centering point, there can be no meaning; with God removed, there is only separation. There is disagreement, disappointment, and division even between father and child, brother and sister, friend and neighbor. People no longer really speak to one another with any assurance of acceptance or respect or security in Babel. We don't understand each other; we thrust ourselves outside the Garden of Eden.

Do you see the power of the grace-gift of God through Jesus precisely in this situation? That life of love was lived in compassion and justice calling us home to unity. The Holy Spirit of God was offered now to engage us in reunion and peace and mission — the Pentecost gift. Look at the grace-gifts within our own gardens.

In her essay titled, *In Search of Our Mothers' Gardens*, Alice Walker wrote:

> *In the late 1920s, my mother ran away from home to marry my father. Marriage, if not running away, was expected of seventeen-year-old girls. By the time she was twenty, she had two children and was pregnant with a third. Five children later, I was born. And this is how I came to know my mother: she seemed a large, soft, loving-eyed woman who was rarely impatient in our home. Her quick, violent temper was on view only a few times a year, when she battled with the white landlord who had the misfortune to suggest to her that her children did not need to go to school.*
>
> *She made all the clothes we wore, even my brother's overalls. She made all the towels and sheets we used. She spent the summers canning vegetables and fruits. She spent the winter evenings making quilts enough to cover all our beds.*
>
> *During the "working" day, she labored beside — not behind — my father in the fields. Her day began before sunup, and did not end until late at night. There was never a moment for her to sit down, undisturbed, to unravel her own private thoughts; never a time free from interruption — by work or the noisy inquiries of her many children....*
>
> *But when, you will ask, did my overworked mother have time to know or care about feeding the creative spirit? (her garden) ... my mother adorned with flowers whatever shabby house we were forced to live in. And not just your typical straggly country stand of zinnias, either. She planted ambitious gardens — and still does — with over fifty different varieties of plants that bloom profusely....*

Whatever she planted grew as if by magic, and her
fame as a grower of flowers spread over three counties.
Because of her creativity with her flowers, even my
memories of poverty are seen through a screen of blooms
— sunflowers, petunias, roses, dahlias, forsythia....
And I remember people coming to my mother's yard
to be given cuttings from her flowers; I hear again the
praise showered on her because whatever rocky soil
she landed on, she turned into a garden. A garden so
brilliant with colors, so original in its design, so mag-
nificent with life and creativity, that to this day people
drive by our house in Georgia — perfect strangers and
imperfect strangers — and ask to stand or walk among
my mother's art.
I notice that it is only when my mother is working
in her flowers that she is radiant, almost to the point of
being invisible — except as Creator: hand and eye. She
is involved in work her soul must have. Ordering the
universe in the image of her personal conception of
Beauty.
Her face, as she prepares the Art that is her gift, is
a legacy of respect she leaves to me, for all that illumi-
nates and cherishes life. She had handed down respect
for the possibilities — and the will to grasp them.
Guided by my heritage of a love of beauty and a
respect for strength — the search of my mother's gar-
den — I found my own.[1]

The garden is a way to give us a specific image around which to study our individual histories, beginning today perhaps with the influence of our mothers. It is not about gardening but about growth into wholeness.

I read a book for this sermon written by a number of feminist theologians who speak out of a number of different cultural backgrounds from all over the world with different languages, yet the garden was one setting that they could all use to define themselves and their unity in Christ.

The image of the garden can be both positive and negative. For some, garden walls were confining, some of the gardens we inherited are colored by destructive factors like racism or classism, or maybe represent various kinds of suffering and oppression, perhaps family violence, alcoholism, divorce, poverty, or sickness, all separated, scattered outside of Eden, beyond the plain of Shinar. For others, their garden heritage has been a mixed bouquet, with flowers but also with weeds; but gardens are intended to be life-affirming — life-sustaining — assisting us to make critical choices in regard to our own journeys — Spirit led.

Poet Stanley Kunitz was asked about his inspiration: He said "gardening." And how does a poet garden? Mostly by caring: "Gardening for me is a passionate effort to organize a little corner of the earth, which I want to redeem." Can we sense the Spirit of God — the counselor — active through some of those who formed who we are today, when God's image shines through?

Digging in one's own garden, one should seek the gifts we have received and now can offer, and what parts of your garden might have been harmful to you and to others? The hope is to find a way to grow that offers wholeness to others that is Spirit led. How to have a global garden as partners, rather than as exploiters of one another, within the goal of clearing away the blight and making space so that we may all grow into the whole human beings that God created us to be.

In the book, *Inheriting Our Mothers' Gardens*, one woman from Cuba wrote,

> *Often when I disagree with my mother, she gets upset, because she thinks I do not value her way of thinking and the way she has lived. But that is not true. To see things differently, and even to think that the way my mother has acted in certain situations is not the way I would act, is in no way a judgment of her. I have a different perspective and have had very different experiences. As a matter of fact, I think the difference exists in part because what she has told me, and the way she has lived has pushed me a few steps farther ... she gave me growth; like her, I believe that apart from community we cannot be about the work of God....* [2]

A woman from El Salvador wrote:

> *This year I have witnessed the beauty that has come forth from (my mother's) garden; the variety of colors, shapes, and designs. I thought of my mother's tiny gardens in city barrios. I now understand much more clearly; gardening is about visioning. It is about faith ... patience, beauty, and sharing. Gardening is about dreaming and futuring. It is one of my mother's legacies to me.[3]*

A professor at Yale Divinity School wrote:

> *Each summer I went to visit my grandmother and followed her about the hot, dusty garden, watering, cutting, and weeding, not because I had come to like gardening but because I loved her.[4]*

Jesus told the disciples in today's text from Saint John, "I am going to God who sent me, but the Holy Spirit of God is offered to you." It is the grace-gift of forgiveness and love. The barriers can fall, and we can again speak the same language.

Here is the heart of Pentecost — gift of the Holy Spirit as the center unity of God, the breath-touch of God; the presence of Christ; the directing, unifying God-force in all existence, the directing heart of what we should be together — mother and child, friend and neighbor, sister and brother, husband and wife. The truth is that you and I are eternally important, eternally loved, eternally accepted, not because of the towers that we have built or the gardens we have tended, but often in spite of them. The spirit of God is that which brings into balance, unites, and calls us home.

This Pentecost, birthday of the church, Parents' Weekend, or Mother's Day, it is time to plant the annuals and to celebrate the perennials. It is time to dig in the soil of our own heritage, and also to accept the gift of the sacred seed and life and faith that grows there.

In the light of Christ, may we all view life as an opportunity for servanthood and reform. May all of us be called into assertive peacemaking and justice-giving; not afraid to challenge and eliminate prejudice. May we be called to be people of dialogue, empathy, respect, and joy, all of which derive from God's grace-gift of faith imaged as the burning word-flame of the Holy Spirit.

Guided by this heritage of love and respect and forgiveness and promise and resurrection, in search of our mother's garden, may we find our own. Amen.

Sermon delivered May 14, 1989
Weaver Chapel
Wittenberg University
Springfield, Ohio

---

1. Alice Walker, *In Search of Our Mothers' Gardens* (San Diego: Harcourt Brace Jovanovich Publishers, 1983), pp. 238-239, 241-243.

2. Letty M. Russell, *Inheriting Our Mothers' Gardens: Feminist Theology in Third World Perspectives* (Philadelphia: Westminster Press, 1988), p. 100.

3. *Ibid*, p. 131.

4. *Ibid*, p. 146.

The Holy Trinity
John 3:1-17

How Can One Be Three?

*Jesus spoke to Nicodemus about the interactive Spirit
of God the creator. Nicodemus replied, "How can these
things be true?"*

*Jesus answered, "We testify to what we have seen;
yet you do not believe our testimony. If I have told you
about earthly things and you don't believe, how can
you believe if I tell you about heavenly things?"*
— John 3:8-12 (paraphrased)

It's Trinity Sunday. I can read your mind. "Oh no! It's the last
Sunday in May, the beginning of tenth week; we are fatigued; what
little gray matter is still functioning needs to be placed in reserve
for finals; please not a sermon on the doctrine of the Trinity!" We
are too tired to play mind games. "The Father is infinite; the Son is
infinite; the Holy Spirit is infinite."

"Nicodemus replied, 'How can these things be true?' "

The Holy Trinity. The very topic brings back memories of confirmation classes past — a pastor desperately looking for a glim-
mer of interest in the eyes of a lethargic class of thirteen-year-olds.
Looking, pleading, the pastor says, slowly, "The Trinity — one
God but three persons — Father, Son, and Holy Spirit — creator,
redeemer, sanctifier." And the eyes of the students were empty.
The students were waiting — catatonic — just waiting for the hour
to be over.

Alister McGrath, who teaches historical and systematic theology at Oxford University and who wrote a book titled, *Understanding the Trinity*, once began a lecture on the topic of the Trinity by
saying, "One of the most vivid memories of my youth involves
being in church and reciting the Athanasian Creed. We got to the

25

bit that reads, 'The Father incomprehensible, the Son incomprehensible, and the Holy Spirit incomprehensible.' And then the young man sitting next to me muttered, too loudly for comfort, 'The whole damn thing is incomprehensible!' "[1]

Nicodemus added, "How can these things be true?"

I talked to some of you and other students at Wittenberg about the doctrine of the Trinity, asking you to remember the various ways your confirmation or Sunday school teachers struggled to explain to you, wiggling in your seats, the concept of the Trinity — Three as one, and one as Three — the one God-force of existence, revealed in three forms. How was it explained to you?

One student remembered the egg illustration — told to the class with an actual egg for visual reinforcement. God is one unity, like one hard-boiled egg, but formed (as the priest cracked the egg open), but formed of three distinct parts — shell, yolk, and albumen. Eyes didn't glaze over in that class, but stomachs were turned thinking of God coming as albumen, or in all that yolky cholesterol desiring to clog your arteries.

How can one God be experienced in three distinct forms?

Another student remembered the apple illustration: One apple and yet three distinct parts — the outer skin, the inner white juicy meat, and the seed core — each serving a different purpose but one apple.

And there is the chocolate-covered peanut M&M illustration.

Yet another student told me one I had not heard before: "The Trinity is like a cherry pie illustration." She said, "The crust contains it all — the cherries have real material substance — and the red filling flows out all over the plate and onto your fingers like the Holy Spirit coming to you personally."

We decided such images of God as apple cores and eggshells probably drove more young confirmands into paganism and agnosticism than into any Trinitarian revelations, sort of like that scene in the film *Nuns on the Run*. An escaped convict masquerading as a nun is forced to teach a confirmation class, but he gets the traditional symbolism a bit confused. Teaching the class about the Trinity, he said that God is like a three-leaf clover — small, green, and a weed, or something like that.

26

"How can these things be true?"

There is the Philadelphia Trinity house explanation: So-called Trinity houses were first built ironically when deism captured the imagination of colonial intellectuals such as Franklin and Jefferson. Trinity houses were tall, narrow, stone row houses. One house but formed of three floors — kitchen level, living room level, and bedroom level — each serving differently the needs of those who lived within but one home. (It has more promise than the cherry pie illustration!)

There is the classic example of the masks of God: One powerful life and future, but experienced by us in the divine wearing different masks of expression — the mask of creation; the mask of human form — Jesus; and the mask of inspiration and compassion imbedded within our own heart of community as Spirit. For Tertullian, who first stated this illustration, the word "person" was connected to a role in a drama. (The Latin word *persona* originally meant "mask.") A Roman actor wore different masks to represent the different characters that he or she portrayed. The Trinitarian concept of "one God in three persons" means one force of action — appearing in different forms — creator, redeemer, sanctifier — yet all played by the same actor — the one God-force of loving.

I like that illustration, but today, "masks" also carry the image of deception.

Perhaps the best illustration remembered by a student: God as total personhood. Think of your own parents — your mother, for example. She is a mother and a wife and to her colleagues perhaps, a lawyer. One loving person (hopefully loving!) — one personhood, but experienced as mother, wife, and legal counsel, yet the same person, but *encountered* in different ways, in different situations.

There was a time once when Christians became really emotional about the concept of the Trinity and demanded to know: How can there be one God when we talk about distinct differences between the Father, Jesus Christ, and the Holy Spirit? Doesn't the Trinity push us into some form of Pantheism? Three in one and one in three.

Nicodemus said, "How can these things be?"

27

But such emotion and expressed confusion is not the problem today. Actually there are two problems today. First, many people just don't believe in, or care about, God (in whatever form) today. Many share the belief of science superstar, Francis Crick, as outlined in his book, *The Astonishing Hypothesis.* Crick wrote that there is no God nor any ultimate meaning to our life together. Our joys and sorrows, memories and ambitions, our sense of personal identity and free will, are in fact no more than the behavior of a vast assembly of nerve cells and their associated molecules.

"How can these things be true?"

Our dialogue with such people is critical today. It's part of our call as highly educated Christians in this postmodern age. And a Trinitarian view of God can best be understood by our contemporary, non-Christian neighbors. But in our assigned text, Nicodemus was a person who did believe in God.

The second problem group we encounter each day are the ones I want us to consider on this Trinity Sunday. Most of the people that we know are like Nicodemus and believe in some sort of God. Today most of those we know probably would consider themselves to be Christians, but many of them also, unknowingly, fracture the Trinitarian formula into separate components, and latch onto just one of these expressions of God. I believe they miss the total call of God, and in so doing further distort their own humanity.

For example, I have known here at Wittenberg a student I will call "A." If asked about his belief in God, student "A" would probably look at you strangely for a moment, wondering why anyone would ask such a strange, irrelevant question, but would eventually respond by admitting that "Yes, sure" he believes in some grand creator — some God. But he has given up church, for one thing.

For him, fellowship at the moment is found in softball and beer and friends at the house. Being "whole" is an issue of medical science. Mention love to him, and he thinks of sex. His concept of death is pretty vague, "When you gotta go, you gotta go" but he doesn't like to think about such things that have the ring of failure. His plan for after graduation is to try whatever works; beat the red tape; avoid long lines; learn what the public wants and either do it or sell it to them.

He is, of course, more complex than this. Friendship is important to him, perhaps also his family. But it appears that at the heart of things his hope and future is precariously balanced on his own production, his own producing of events and opportunities. It is a fragile future, even self-destructive because it's not hooked into the due process of caring love and responsibility, or the universal unity of God's forgiveness and grace. There is no apparent realization of the availability of the Holy Spirit or of Jesus as the Christ "in, with, and under" the hidden lives that we touch or touch us.

Student "A" claims a belief in God, but his only perceived experience of God is God as the creative source of existence — the prime mover and cosmic mystery — a God who is distant, impersonal, some master machinist far removed from the human relationships of day-to-day living. It is not the God who comes to meet us where we are.

The Trinity has been fractured. The creative source alone (God the Father in traditional terms) bears only partial resemblance to the God who is described throughout scripture and within Christian experience.

For student "B," Rwanda and Haiti have their effect — the injustice is overwhelmingly obvious. She's also very concerned about the quality of the water forming our nearby Buck Creek, all those herbicides and pesticides are fertilizers washing off the Reid Park golf course; and the impact a trash-burning incinerator would have on local air quality. But she often feels alone in her concerns, in her anger. Why does she feel so strongly about those issues of the quality of life? Who else cares? What difference does it all make anyway?

I don't think that she realizes that she is in tune with the very "itinerary of creation by God" — the intended harmony and stability. Her will for justice would fit well within the peace of God as lived by Jesus and desired by the active Spirit of God. Here is the ultimate reason for her struggle for righteousness.

She doesn't see the divine connection to her concern, nor her connection with other Christians. She feels so alone, angry, and frustrated. "Who cares?" she wonders. The Trinity is fractured.

29

Or there is student "C" who claims Jesus as her personal Savior. There is a future offered her and she knows it. She seems to care only about those who are just like her in her beliefs and cultural expression. She forms clear distinctions between secular matter and spiritual matters. She, too, has lost the unity of the Trinity. She sees Jesus as the Christ, touching lepers, feeding the hungry, praising the Samaritan, talking responsibility to the temple and government authorities, accepting, loving, and healing the whole neighborhood. She has missed the gift of God as universal creator, Savior, and engaging Holy Spirit.

It is Trinity Sunday. It may seem to some as an outdated festival but its message is at the heart of our Christian confession. The God revealed in the Trinity formula holds our life together.

Nicodemus asked, "How can these things be true?" Jesus said, "We speak of what we have experienced; we testify to what we have seen...."

The Trinity is where earthly and heavenly things merge in life-sustaining love for each one of us.

I end this sermon in the name of the Father, and of the Son, and of the Holy Spirit: God as loving parent, sustainer of the totality of meaningful reality.

God as the Son — the Christ — God coming into our own history, having lived our pain and fear, and our joy and peace. The Son is God walking with us — the story of love intersecting our stories and sharing even our death and still offering us more.

God as Spirit — the Holy Spirit — God's daily offer of help and hope; the power of loving transformation. The Holy Spirit is God penetrating all our depths — all the psychological layering of our selves, and all our times and places, and offering peace.

Father, Son, and Holy Spirit — one God of love.

Sermon delivered May 29, 1994
Weaver Chapel
Wittenberg University
Springfield, Ohio

1. Alister McGrath, *Understanding the Trinity* (Grand Rapids, Michigan: Zondervan Publishing Company, 1988).

Betting On Foolish Pleasure

*"Not everyone who says to me, 'Lord, Lord,' will enter
the kingdom of heaven, but only the one who does the
will of my Father in heaven. On that day many will say
to me, 'Lord, Lord, did we not prophesy in your name,
and cast out demons in your name, and do many deeds
of power in your name?' Then I will declare to them, 'I
never knew you; go away from me, you evildoers.' Everyone then who hears these words of mine and acts on
them will be like a wise man who built his house on
rock. The rain fell, the floods came, and the winds blew
and beat on that house, but it did not fall, because it
had been founded on rock. And everyone who hears
these words of mine and does not act on them will be
like a foolish man who built his house on sand. The
rain fell, and the floods came, and the winds blew and
beat against that house, and it fell — and great was its
fall!" Now when Jesus had finished saying these things,
the crowds were astounded at his teaching.*
— Matthew 7:21-28

*"When the Son of Man comes in his glory, and all the
angels with him, then he will sit on the throne of his
glory. All the nations will be gathered before him, and
he will separate people one from another as a shepherd separates the sheep from the goats, and he will
put the sheep at his right hand and the goats at the left.
Then the king will say to those at his right hand, 'Come,
you that are blessed by my Father, inherit the kingdom
prepared for you from the foundation of the world; for
I was hungry and you gave me food, I was thirsty and
you gave me something to drink, I was a stranger and*

33

you welcomed me, I was naked and you gave me clothing, I was sick and you took care of me, I was in prison and you visited me.' Then the righteous will answer him, 'Lord, when was it that we saw you hungry and gave you food, or thirsty and gave you something to drink? And when was it that we saw you a stranger and welcomed you, or naked and gave you clothing? And when was it that we saw you sick or in prison and visited you?' And the king will answer them, 'Truly I tell you, just as you did it to one of the least of these who are members of my family, you did it to me.' Then he will say to those at his left hand, 'You that are accursed, depart from me into the eternal fire prepared for the devil and his angels; for I was hungry and you gave me no food, I was thirsty and you gave me nothing to drink, I was a stranger and you did not welcome me, naked and you did not give me clothing, sick and in prison and you did not visit me.' Then they also will answer, 'Lord, when was it that we saw you hungry or thirsty or a stranger or naked or sick or in prison, and did not take care of you?' Then he will answer them, 'Truly I tell you, just as you did not do it to one of the least of these, you did not do it to me.' " — Matthew 25:31-45

Grace to you and peace from God our Father and the Lord Jesus Christ.

This year's Kentucky Derby was run just a few weeks ago. I am sure that since that time, the race has been analyzed from many angles in regard to speed, handicapping, condition of the track, and the riding maneuvers of the various jockeys.

I read a letter to the editor in a news magazine this week that also implied a little different type of insight into the race — sort of a symbolic theological insight. I don't particularly like horse racing, but I enjoy symbolic insights, so I checked this one out, and it seems to be accurate.

Apparently in the recent running of the Kentucky Derby, two horses were fighting for the lead, neck and neck; but in the midst of their combat, a third horse came up from behind and stole the purse. The two horses intent on only challenging each other for the lead position were named Avatar and Diabolo.

Avatar is an ancient Sanskrit word meaning "he who passes or goes beyond — come down." In the Hindu religion, it means a god coming down in bodily form to the earth; it means the incarnation of god — the meaning of existence coming into human life.

The other horse in the early neck-and-neck battle for the roses was named Diabolo. This name has its origin in the Greek word *diabolos* that means simply "the devil," the inhuman slanderer, the classical power of sin, of innate selfishness, of separation from Avatar, from god incarnate.

While these two horses with their classical, symbolic religious names are battling each other, what horse comes from behind and captures the trophy and the hearts and minds of all the spectators? Good old Foolish Pleasure. To me, this seems very symbolic of our particular culture today.

There are many people who pay lip service to their belief and trust in a god and people who call themselves Christians who claim their ultimate direction and concern has been revealed, made clear by the Christ, by God incarnate, by a particular living Avatar, who also pays lip service to the reality of Diabolo, to the reality of their innate self-imposed separation from God as the power of existence. They claim to sense their sin and need of forgiveness. But for so many, who really is in control, who is the acting god image or idol set up by cheering crowds today? It's foolish pleasure, an ethics of convenience, authority by the self, a personal isolationism.

(In traditional theology, the Kentucky Derby analogy would fall apart because, strictly speaking, Foolish Pleasure would also be a part of Diabolo.) But the question still remains: In our permissive, selfish world today, who really is our authority in the face of Foolish Pleasure?

Our gospel lesson for today is from the conclusion of the Sermon on the Mount as recorded in the book of Matthew. Today's lesson is really in three sections.

The first section draws a distinction between what one says and what one does, or better yet, between what one says and what one is.

Jesus taught them saying, "Not every one who says to me, 'Lord, Lord,' shall enter the kingdom of heaven, but rather he who does (who lives) the will of my Father. Many will say, 'Lord, Lord, we prophesied in your name; we did great works in your name, we went to war in your name, we imprisoned in your name, we built up great industry in your name, we put ourselves as "number one" in your name, we even enshrined "foolish pleasure" in your name and even call ourselves Christians.' And the Christ will declare to them, 'I never knew you!' "   — Matthew 7:21-23 (paraphrased)

The second part of today's lesson draws a similar distinction between a true discipleship and a false, rootless, shallow, proclamation of adhesion.

"Everyone who then hears these words of love and life and does them will be like one building his house upon the rock. One who bases his life on the giving love of the Christ bases his life on the fabric and foundation of existence. And everyone who hears these words of mine and does not do them but builds his house — his being — on egotism and foolish pleasure is like a foolish person who built his house upon the sand; and the rain fell and the floods came, and the winds blew and beat against that house; and it fell; and great was the fall of it."   — Matthew 7:24-25 (paraphrased)

The third part of today's gospel reading, which concludes the Sermon on the Mount, draws a distinction between the authority of Jesus and the opinion of the scribes.

And when Jesus finished these sayings, the crowds were astonished at this teaching, for he taught them as one who had authority, and not as their scribes.
        — Matthew 7:28-29 (paraphrased)

When one's authority is based on the ground of existence, that authority has power over all else, whether planned human power or foolish human pleasure.

Unfortunately, I guess, acting in that authority, doing God's will by building your house on the rock is often not the safest path to take. A foundation of sand in the short run is often safer.

Historically, a good example of the danger of building on the rock of life is the early church leader, Justin. You may have noticed that occasionally in the past few months our opening section of the service from the insert *Celebrate* has recognized the deeds and life of some historical faithful Christians.

When the Protestant church did away with most of the saints' days (in Christ we are all saints and sinners before God), they directed worship toward God who was the authority of the saints.

After this occurrence, in a sense throwing out the saints, unless one studied history in detail or theology, many of these courageous and faithful early Christians were forgotten. Remembering them now on their traditional birth or death day in *Celebrate* and in the church calendar year helps to fill in this historical gap.

Justin was born about 100 AD of wealthy pagan parents and became well educated in Greek philosophy. On his conversion to Christianity he traveled from place to place, like other professional philosophers, writing and lecturing on the truth, in this case, of Christian belief. He was lecturing against the foolish pleasures, the misused and ill-directed powers, the selfish actions and the religious myths of the Roman empire and the Greek mentality of the second century AD. He was executed by government order, in Rome, in about 165 AD.

I think we have to almost as dramatically take our stand against false gods and foolish pleasure today.

At the recent New Jersey Synod Convention, many such stands were taken and adopted by our church. I think a prime example of a stand that was taken and must be taken in the name of Christ was a resolution on world hunger.

The convention statement put it this way: "Because the crisis of world hunger needs to be acted upon on many different levels, the New Jersey Synod in Convention calls upon the individual members of its congregations to pray and to seek guidance as to how *each person* might make an impact upon this great tragedy of world hunger, to reorder their lifestyles in order to conserve resources so that people might be fed, to reevaluate habits of consumption relevant to the scarcity of energy, fertilizers, and water resources including the minimization of our horrible wastefulness in consumption, to take initiative to set up and participate in viable programs that will help increase the world food supply."

If you think about it, this is a direct attack upon both foolish pleasure and *diabolos*. It is a cry for a new responsible lifestyle, one that respects the preciousness of all humans, of all people. It is a call for a global consciousness and a global living here and now. As the relative wealthy, we have to end our long ego trip and see our part in God's total earthly family. We have to dare the new lifestyle in close support of all life.

God is the source of love's power and love demands justice. Dignity, pride, laughter, joy; these feelings are common to all humanity, to the whole person. Hunger is opposed to this unity of the whole person. Hunger is unjust and opposed to God's intention for a life together in love.

We talk about a new mentality, a new lifestyle, a new global awareness. It's really not that new.

Toward the end of the book of Matthew, there is a section that in many ways parallels today's Matthian readings from the Sermon on the Mount. In this later section from Matthew 25:31-45, in a symbolic, futuristic setting, so the story goes, all the earth's people are divided into two groups.

> *And the power of life says to one group, "Come and receive the kingdom which has been prepared for you even since the creation of the world. I was hungry and you fed me, thirsty and you gave me drink; I was a stranger and you received me in your homes, naked and you clothed me; I was sick and you took care of me, in prison and you visited me." And the surprised group will say, "When did we ever see you a stranger and welcome you in our homes, or naked and clothed you?" The king will answer back, "I tell you, indeed, whenever you did this for one of the least important of these my brother and sisters of the world, you did it for me." Then the power of life will say to those on his left,*

"Away from me ... I was hungry but you would not feed me, thirsty but you would not give me drink; I was sick and in prison but you would not take care of me." Then they will answer him, "When, Lord, did we ever see you hungry, or thirsty, or a stranger, or naked, or sick, or in prison, and we would not help you?" The king will answer them back, "I tell you, indeed, whenever you refused to help one of these least important ones, you refused to help me."

— Matthew 25:34-45 (paraphrased)

I think this is the ultimate of global awareness — it is the awareness of life. The Christ is the one who brings life, who brings the direction of God, who bases your house on the bedrock of meaningful existence.

Foolish pleasure or arrogant egotism is a house on sand. We ask help to base our lives in the ultimate authority of Jesus as the Christ as we reach out our hands in love to our hungry neighbors.

May the peace of God, which passes all understanding, keep our hearts and minds through Christ Jesus. In Christ's name we pray. Amen.

Sermon delivered on June 1, 1975
Resurrection Lutheran Church
Hamilton Square, New Jersey

39

Pentecost 2/Baccalaureate
Isaiah 44:21-25; Psalm 81:1-3, 6-10;
2 Corinthians 4:5-12; Mark 2:23-28

What's In Your Wallet?

Out of darkness the light shall shine! God's glory shin-
ing in the face of Christ. Yet we who have this spiritual
gift are like common clay pots.
— 2 Corinthians 4:6-7 (paraphrased)

Here's the scene: Two women are sitting together at a table in
an inner-city shelter. One is a street person, quite drunk, in torn
layers of tattered clothes, unwashed hair in disarray, talking loudly
to the other woman about something that seems to the speaker to
be of critical importance yet seems like nonsense to the casual ob-
server. The second woman is Dorothy Day, who at this point in her
career is quite famous, as a founder of the Catholic Worker Movement. Day sits with the other woman and listens carefully to her
story. They are soon joined by a man, a reporter, who stands there,
impatiently, waiting for a pause in the alcoholic ranting, to inter-
view Day. It was all quite obvious, the purpose of his presence.
After a while, Day politely asks her companion if she may please
interrupt their conversation for a moment. Day then looks at the
man and asks, "Are you waiting to talk with one of us?" With one
of us. Not to "me" but to one of us sacred human beings — bag
woman or famous, educated social reformer. Are you waiting to
talk with one of us in the equality of our capacity for pain or joy,
for disintegration or loving balance? Do you wish to speak to one
of us?

The God who said, "Out of darkness the light shall shine!" is
the same God who made this light shine in our hearts — God's
glory shining in the face of Christ. Yet we who are offered this

41

spiritual gift are like common clay pots, like earthenware vessels — fragile flesh and blood and self-realized, finite beings, yet to whom has been offered good news — a final word that holds no finale, offered to us, such fragile humanity, in the freedom of our decisions — earthenware, yet sacred.

"Do you want to speak to one of us?" Common clay yet so uniquely valuable. What is it that forms that kind of a perception so grounded in both humility and respect? Life that so easily flows into servanthood and accountability?

The baccalaureate sermon is traditionally the final word of the school's pastor to the graduating class. It is my final, formal prayer for you — a hope that you will easily and knowingly hook into eternal reality.

Dorothy Day once said, "Accountability means that one has lived in such a way that one's life would not make sense if God did not exist."

In addition to being baccalaureate weekend, it is also my re-union weekend at Wittenberg — a twenty year class reunion; and as I composed this homily for our seniors, it has become not only advice, hope, and a prayer for you who are about to graduate, but it also has taken the form of an introspective interrogation, an asking of myself if I have followed my own advice and hope for you. I see myself twenty years ago in you seniors, and I wonder about my own faithfulness in terms of accountability over these past twenty years.

I was given a new wallet for my birthday this year. The old wallet was beginning to crack at the creases and rip at the seams. It probably would have had its twentieth anniversary this year, too, but it didn't quite make it. It has been a faithful wallet. It never lost itself over the years, never allowed itself to be forcefully taken by anyone else. It was there when I needed it. It traveled with me, close to the hip, through good times and bad. Gathered up each morning off the bureau in a blurry-eyed routine, it went to the office with me and into hospitals and classrooms, and through customs into other countries, and stayed skin-close through soaking rains, and while bicycling and hiking.

42

Clothes would change, shoes would wear out, pens would disappear, but this wallet remained faithful. Sure, once in a while I would prune it, updating cards and photos. It never did hold on to money very well. But one's wallet is more than an accessory. A wallet is a container of one's life and values and priorities, holding snugly symbols and images of self and hope and pretension.

After the new birthday wallet was presented, all stiff and arrogant and new, the old wallet had to be emptied in a solemn ceremony one evening — its contents laid out with formality on a clear surface. It was like some mystical autopsy, like dying and having the contents of one's soul, the interior of one's living, exposed on some heavenly bureau for final examination. I mean, what is it that I kept so close to me, to identify my being? What were the essentials in such a tiny, finite container held so intimately? What pieces of paper and plastic give testimony to who I am or wish to be?

I found hidden in my old wallet a membership card to a New Jersey tennis club that expired in 1978. How did that card survive? Why did it remain? A reminder of past locations and experiences now not to be forgotten? I do vaguely remember thinking to myself that this card will remind me that I should play tennis again. I need the exercise. It would be good for me — mind, soul, and body. This card was to be a constant reminder. But I haven't played tennis in ten years. Am I trying to deceive myself? What other promises have I not kept? What promises to yourself are you not going to keep, seniors? What more important promises of personal integrity, not to be kept?

There was a short stack of credit cards to stores I never get to, and bank cards with three dimensional eagles flapping their wings, representing a credit status that sets me apart — that distances me from so many others, a wedge between me and their struggle for the necessities that I too often take for granted. A stack of plastic cards in good standing to meet my reasonable wants, but do I want a decent life for these others, for all others?

"Do you want to speak to one of us?" I found a tattered list of books, titles, and authors, a "must read" list for, who knows, when I might stumble upon a used bookstore, or be stuck in a city or on some distant campus while in the money and mood to do some serious shopping; and I can then whip out this crumbled list that was apparently updated sometime early last August. (It has salt water and suntan lotion stains.) There are 29 book titles, and only a few of those have been crossed off; only four from this particular list actually acquired and read since last summer. Many of the other 25 are important to me. Where does the time and the mental energy go? Will you seniors be better time managers? Time for what?

There is a sky blue Ohio Bell, "America's Calling Card" with a 13-digit international number, the miracle of modern communication, but what does one say? "Sorry, I must miss your birthday/anniversary/graduation. I just don't have the time right now," or "I want this from you"? Always, "I want this from you." Or do you say things like, "I miss you, I care, what can I do for you to help?" What does one say with a sky-blue calling card?

There was my AAA card for travel security. And my Social Security card (with a number that is impossible to memorize). But what does it mean to be "secure"?

There was my uniform donor card that has printed on it, "In the hope that I may help others, I hereby make this anatomical gift, if medically acceptable, to take effect upon my death." (One's death is easily accepted at age 21, seemingly centuries away.) Now, like my old wallet, at my twentieth anniversary reunion, I feel a little cracked at the creases, stretched at the seams. Twenty years, and look what happened to my old wallet, buried now, in a bureau drawer six inches under a layer of dark socks!

"I hereby make this anatomical gift, to take effect upon my death. I give any needed organs or parts for the purpose of transplantation, therapy, medical research or education, in the hope that it will help others."

It's an old ragged card, actually signed and dated not too long after my graduation, now confirmed on the back of my current driver's license. But at death, my body becomes a gift, if appropriate for use. A card as a humble expression of my faith, the card of an earthenware container, but, "Out of darkness the light shall shine," Saint Paul wrote.

There was my Delta Dental plan card, and my university Medical Benefits identification insurance card — "All hospital and surgical benefits are paid directly to the provider of care," and my health plan identification card — "Prior to hospital admission, or within 72 hours of emergency admission, notify the plan's coordinator. Failure to call will reduce your benefits." In the last twenty years, I have been in a lot of hospitals to visit parishioners and students or to study the justice of health care from the computerized, high-tech university research hospitals to primitive co-op clinics in Third World nations, and in each location talked to people who had no one to call for any kind of real assistance. They had no real benefits to reduce. How can I, or you, alter this disparity?

There, too, was my voter registration card with precinct #30, which I can also never remember, but which ties me into a system, even though, it seems, that the candidates I vote for always lose. It is often not even close. The quality of life throughout the world is deeply influenced, positively and often negatively, by the decisions made by our governmental system of which we are a part, called to be a responsible part and change agent of the system. But remember also when Jesus was walking through some wheat fields on a sabbath; he picked the wheat. When should we, too, break the custom or law to feed the hungry, for example? The sabbath was made for the good of humanity; respect for God and loving service are entwined. "Compassion and love, not the blind observation of regulations, are to form the expression of the Christian life." That is the gospel reading for this Sunday (Mark 2:23-28 reworded).

Now this is bizarre; at the time of my twentieth year class reunion, stuck between two other cards in my old wallet was my SSR form, number 2, and my old notice of draft classification. My selective service registration certificate, with my selective service number and a list of obvious physical characteristics — height and weight and blue eyes registered with the local board, number 33 for New Jersey, third floor, Bangs Avenue, Asbury Park. "Any person who alters, forges, or in any manner changes this certificate may be fined not to exceed $10,000 or imprisoned for not more than five years, or both. The law requires you to have this certificate in your personal possession at all times and to notify your local draft board in writing within ten days of marital, family, or dependency status."

At commencement twenty years ago, that little card allowed some of us to go on to graduate schools, some to various occupations, and placed others of us on a fast tract, as Second Lieutenants, to Vietnam, a college liberal arts education making us leaders of others, leading some of us through jungles where Second Lieutenants had the highest fatality rate of any rank, shot in both the front and the back.

I went to graduate school and protest rallies against the war but never burned the card. I kept it safe in my wallet, mixing guilt and action, risk and compromise, which has not ended along with the constant stream of justice issues where lives are being belittled or cut short. How afar does one go to spill out one's conviction in action? So I write to South Africa demanding information and release for certain prisoners of conscience, and then write on the same computer disk to other officials within the same governmental structure to recommend black students for graduate school within South Africa; or to seek politely an exit visa for other black, South African nationals. But how do my dual actions in that computerized system of fear and suspicion assist in offering freedom to some and injustice to others? Does my desire for liberation cause additional pain? It's not just a matter of my personal sacrifice (which is very little), and which in some ways would be the easy action to take, but it always involves others. Sometimes that leads into an intense internal struggle, like going to rallies but keeping the card safe in one's wallet, an inner struggle, but, "God said, 'Remember this, I created you to be my servant ...' " (Isaiah 44:21 paraphrased).

I found an instant winner ticket for a Big Mac sandwich that is probably no longer valid but if it is, whether I eat it in or take it out, it is served in a styrofoam container that has and will, with thousands of others, wreak havoc on the environment. But I am very fond of Big Macs. So I write Ronald and ask, "Why don't you put them in a paper container, like Burger King does?" Though I write to Burger King also to remind them that their fish sandwich is supporting the Icelandic fishing industry that operates at the moment in flagrant violation of the International Whaling Commission moratorium on killing whales. I do believe that even these little pesky items speak to the "why" of our earthenware life together — the "us" of living, rather than just looking out for "me."

So there were membership cards in the Sierra Club, Bread for the World, Amnesty International, cards that really serve no purpose in one's wallet, representing organizations of human limitation, but also, for me, symbols of the way the world should be — in harmony. In traditional terms, they hold in my mind hope for the kingdom of God. "Shout for joy, you mountains, and every tree of the forest. I God alone stretched out the heavens" (Isaiah 44:23-24 paraphrased).

I have pictures of my wife and children, certainly something I didn't have in my wallet at the time of my graduation; though it was, I believe, tucked away nicely in my expectations and aspirations. In my case (and there are other equally blessed arrangements), there was the hope for a spouse and children to love and care for, and to receive love and care from, as well as to offer, in all its incompleteness, my will for unity forever. I hope you know what I mean, in this age of temporary promise, when I say a will for unity *forever.*

I have shown these pictures from my wallet to people I meet in fast-paced inner cities or in the countryside in Nicaragua and Jordan and India, and they convey, in a way that these people pictured, this woman and these children, their well-being and future, are very important to me. Other people often show me their pictures, or their children; and I see my children and my spouse in the eyes of those they love. We understand each other for a moment and the way life should be for us all, forever; it is earthenware but something more, willing peace and resurrection.

There is a card identifying me as an ordained pastor, granting me access to strange intensive care units and emergency rooms at distant hospitals. This card that means to me vocation, grounded in a faith commitment. I hope that the card you carry in your wallet to identify your occupational status will also convey to you the same sense of vocation, accountable to the God who said, "Out of darkness the light shall shine."

You see, my baccalaureate prayer for you is that you will feel the pulse beat and breath of that which is grounded in permanent safety — that which offers a model for living in compassion, expressed in servanthood and respect, that renews rather than just consumes.

I hope that you will be peacemakers between family members and maybe even between nations. I wish future homes and families of stability and safety for you. I wish you a setting where love can flow and there can be joy supported by trust, where promises are covenantal and, to the very best of your ability, kept. I wish for you a personal ethic of "love seeking justice."

I want from you protection for the good earth. And I want for you in the center of your being, in your living and relating, a balance that enables you to peer over barriers of relating — a balance that enables you to peer over barriers of difference formed by language and culture, time and space, race and belief, wealth and privilege, and be able to perceive a divine will for unity, not division. "Do you want to talk with one of us, all of us being sacred?"

I want for you moral sensitivity, empathy, and a realized accountability for your intellectual and economic gifts. That life does not have to be lived as though it is a competition between some who win and some who lose; there are ways to achieve objectives that are not violent for others, but rather where all can win.

This will often run counter to the way others live and treat each other, but this is not a lifestyle determined by popularity polls. We carry with us in our body the death of Jesus. My baccalaureate hope for you is an intensified image of full humanity, earthenware containers infused with the eternity of love: a self-vision where the power of compassion in community has transcending power — a realization that servanthood and justice, that harmony and peace are all willed and intended by a greater authority than our own self-interest or instinct.

My pastoral hope is that you can even name the source: "God's glory shining in the face of Christ...." a covenant rooted in a love that was actually lived by Jesus and that will never ultimately disappoint.

Common clay containers who welcome this gift and accept the forgiveness — God's glory shining in the face of Christ, in the words of Saint Paul — may be often troubled, but not crushed; sometimes in doubt, but never in despair; there may be enemies, but we are never without a friend; hurt badly at times, but never destroyed, for here is the cradle of eternity, with the fulfilled promise of unity; here is genuine joy and balance — divine synergy.

As today's psalm put it:

> *... start the music and beat the tambourines ... blow the trumpet for the festival ... I, God, took the burdens off your backs; I who brought you out of the land of Egypt. Even from my hiding place in the storm, I answered you.*   — Psalm 81 (paraphrased)

Here, alone is final forgiveness — here, alone is final liberation. So, "... start the music, beat the tambourines, and blow the trumpet for the joyous festival of your future."

Sermon delivered June 5, 1988
Weaver Chapel
Wittenberg University
Springfield, Ohio

Pentecost 3
Psalm 50:12b; 24:1; Genesis 2:15

The Earth Is The Lord's

... the world and all that is in it is mine.
— Psalm 50:12b

The earth is the Lord's and all that is in it.
— Psalm 24:1

The Lord God took the man and put him in the garden of Eden to till it and keep it. — Genesis 2:15

Grace to you and peace from God our Father and the Lord Jesus Christ.

In the beginning God created heaven and earth. He was then immediately faced with a class action lawsuit for failing to file an environmental impact statement with the Cosmic Environmental Protection Agency — an angelically staffed agency dedicated to keeping the universe pollution free. God was granted a temporary permit for the heavenly portion of the project, but was issued a cease and desist order on the earthly part, pending further investigation by The Cosmic Environmental Protection Agency.

Upon completion of his construction permit application and environmental impact statement, God appeared before the council to answer questions. When asked why he began these projects in the first place, God simply replied that he liked to be creative. This was not considered adequate reasoning, and God was required to substantiate this further. The council was unable to see any practical use for earth since "the

51

earth was void and empty and darkness was upon the face of the deep." Then God said, "Let there be light."

God should never have brought up this point. One member of the council immediately protested, asking, "How was the light to be made? Would it involve strip mining? What about thermal pollution? Air pollution?" God explained the light would come from a huge ball of fire.

Nobody on the council really understood this, but it was provisionally accepted assuming there would be no smog or smoke resulting from the ball of fire. A separate burning permit would be required, and since continuous light would be a waste of energy, it should be dark at least one-half of the time.

So God agreed to divide light and darkness and he would call the light Day and the darkness Night. (But the council expressed no interest in in-house semantics.)

When asked how the earth would be covered, God said, "Let there be firmament made amidst the waters; and let it divide the waters from the waters."

One council member accused God of double talk, but the council tabled action since God would be required first to file for a permit from the Angelic Bureau of Land Management and further would be required to obtain water permits from appropriate agencies.

The council asked if there would be only water and firmament and God said, "Let the earth bring forth the green herb and such as may seed, and the fruit tree yielding fruit after its kind." The council agreed, as long as native seed would be used.

About future development, God also said, "Let the waters bring forth creatures having life and the fowl that may fly over the earth."

Here again, the council took no formal action since this would require approval of the Fish and Game Commission coordinated with the Cosmic Wildlife Federation and Audubongelic Society.

It appeared everything was in order until God stated he wanted to complete the project in six days. At this time he was advised by the council that his timing

was completely out of the question. The Cosmic Environmental Protection Agency would require a minimum of 180 days to review the application and environmental impact statement; then there would be the public hearings. At a minimum, it would take ten to twelve months before a permit could be granted if the proposal was accepted by all parties.
So God said, "Forget it."

This little bit of fantasy titled, "God and the EPA" was read in the US House of Representatives last year by a member from California and recorded in the Congressional Record. A parishioner, Clark Gilman, brought it to my attention.

What is, of course, ironical about this little tale is that if humanity had responded in care and concern about the earth and the life that it supports the way God had intended from the beginning of time, there would have been no need for the various environmental protection agencies today. But centuries of human selfishness have forced such agencies, red tape and all, to be protectors of the world's various life support systems, protectors in many cases of God's intention.

The front and back of our bulletin sets the theme of this sermon, with its quotation from Psalms: "The world and all that is in it is mine." And on the back cover: "The earth is the Lord's."

"The earth is the Lord's," but what have we done to it? Have we been good tenants or responsible stewards?

I clipped out recent articles from newspapers and magazines on *The Bulletin of the Atomic Scientists*, published by a group of scientists who created the atomic bomb, has recorded the imminence of a nuclear holocaust with a "doomsday clock" on its cover. After the US and USSR signed their first nuclear arms limitation pact, the editors set back the clock to twelve minutes to midnight, the farthest it has ever been from that apocalyptic hour. Now the editors are no longer so optimistic. With the lack of a further arms agreement between the superpowers, the continued spread of nuclear weaponry emphasized by India's entry into the "nuclear club," the American promise of reactor technology to the volatile

Middle East, the increasing vulnerability to nuclear sabotage and terrorism by amateur bomb-makers, the clock hands on the bulletin cover have been pushed forward to nine minutes before midnight.

Other articles gave facts. For example, driving an automobile 25 miles at a moderate speed uses up more air than would be breathed by seven million people during the same time period.

DDT has accumulated in the bodies of virtually all living things.

One hundred SST supersonic aircraft flying continuously for 35 years, if present calculations about the ozone layer are accurate, could make the entire ecology of earth resemble the ecology of Venus. In other words: dead.

Another article began by saying, "Dinner everyone — First, imported sardines, then chicken croquettes in white wine sauce, with a few yummies to follow. That's for Samantha. For Buddy, there are flamed medallions of beef and vitamin-enriched doughnuts. Carol's getting fruit treats. Oh, for us and our kids, it's spaghetti again and no meatballs — inflation, remember. But the first three guests eat well — Samantha's the cat, Buddy is a beagle, and Carol is a canary."

Another article last week was about how many hamburgers and other food items McDonald's throws away daily because that food is no longer hot and grill fresh after being mass prepared during the heaviest hours of their business day.

Then our Lutheran Church in America's hunger information states that two-thirds of the world, two-and-a-half billion people are hungry right now, 400 million starving, over 10,000 people will be dead today, and each day due to starvation. How many brains of young children will be ill-developed because of malnutrition?

The bicentennial is a good time to consider ecology. Much is being written and printed on the way things were in our country not that long ago. For example, consider the air and water of New York City and the Hudson River.

Verrazano, who sailed up the river in 1524, noted that the trees exhaled the sweetest odors.

Robert Juet, who sailed with Henry Hudson, noted that sweet smells rose from the grass, flowers, and trees around Manhattan

Island. Later, a Dutch settler noted that what is now Yonkers was a cool and pleasant resting place beside crystal clear waters. But after a few years in a throw away culture, the river is now the home of bottles, cans, rusted refrigerators, washing machines, mattresses, radios, television sets, and the carcasses of dead automobiles.

Misuse of the environment is certainly worldwide, but because our country has always been a world leader industrially and economically in the past 100 years, we also seem to be a world leader in the misuse of our environment.

The US contains only less than 6% of the world's population but consumes almost half of the world's production of natural resources and accounts for over a quarter of the world's air and sea pollution.

But you know the situation. Answers to such complex problems are not easily solved, but they should not be ignored either.

I think there are certainly viable answers within our corporate and personal reach.

Most importantly for this brief sermon, I feel at least, we must as Christians often be reminded of the reason why life — human life and all other forms of earthly life — is important. It's not only a matter of feeling guilty but I do feel we have to sensitize ourselves toward a need for structural change.

I don't think we should feel guilty to the point of just feeling bad, or to the point where we give some money toward world hunger, for example, and then try to feel better.

I have listed some facts of our current situation not to cause guilt but to help us understand the situation and its future. I don't think we should feel guilty but realize that two-thirds of the world's population is not eating properly, and we should use the strength gained from our meal for our job — to care for our families, and to work for worldwide justice politically in regard to hunger or ecology, for example.

Let me now give a very brief theological base to this whole ecology or biology problem. It is a product of human nature and therefore, it requires a moral and, for us, a Christian approach.

Humanity is considered unique in nature; it has been given dominion over the fish of the sea and over the birds of the air and over every living thing. Genesis stated humanity was given the power to name, which meant to control nature.

But there is a real difference between "dominance" and "arrogance" — just as there is a difference between our "use" and "abuse" of nature.

In Genesis, all creation is called good. Genesis stated, "The Lord took man [Adam] and put him in the Garden of Eden in the world to till it and keep it, not carelessly exploit it" (Genesis 2:15 paraphrased).

The early Hebrew saw God as the source of everything that exists, including the natural process that formed a human as a relational being — as a conscious part of nature, as made in the image of God, in the image of the source of everything that exists. We must ask: Is the destruction of our environment by pollution done as one in the image of God the creator, the source of life? A consistent biblical view would say the rest of nature is really our silent brothers and sisters.

When parts of nature die, a part of us dies also; it's a matter of quality. Humankind does not own the world; he is a part of it.

A human is *in* nature and a part of nature; the two cannot be separated. The word "creation" includes both the human and the nonhuman reality. God is not nature but God is in that plan behind all of life. We in our power have the responsibility and the obligation never to use the world's resources for our own selfish interest.

Today's ecology crisis is a combination of ignorance and arrogance — ignorance in not perceiving that the nonhuman world has a God-given integrity of its own, and that we are all interrelated.

Destroying or abusing the environment is like an amputation — we may survive, but we have lost a part of ourselves. The underlying cause of the ecological crisis also stems from our arrogance, our rebellion against God, our alienation from our neighbors; it stems from our selfishness and our sinfulness.

Our God is the ground of all being and becoming and is at the heart of the fabric of the entire cosmos and not only the God of human beings. We are affirming that the universe and our world is a community. Everything is related immediately to God as he creates, unites, and draws all things forward toward his final future.

Within this community, this vast cosmic household, moreover, everything, all the creatures of nature and all the children of humanity, are intricately and essentially related to everything else.

Humans are unique in their freedom and in their participating awareness of God's overall intention but they are also unique in their choice of selfishness; human sinfulness is a radical disruption of the fabric of interrelatedness that God intended to be characteristic of the world.

It is in man's pride, his willfulness, his arrogance, which separates him from God and from his fellow men and also estranges him from his brother, the Earth, and indeed, the entire cosmos.

As Christians, we believe that Jesus as the Christ has shown us the intention of all power and meaning. God is revealed to be intimately close to all his creatures.

In Jesus' freedom for others, in his ability and willingness to give himself in love and to receive love in return, Jesus has shown the divine intention that a human is to be a responsible being.

Our innate selfishness is forgiven and we have been set free to be God's servants in the world and to be faithful to God's purposes; being faithful to God's purposes includes both the care of the Earth and the responsibility to see that all people are enabled to fulfill their humanity as God's children. Both of these are involved in our environmental crisis.

We ask that the promised hope of fulfillment in God's wholeness seen through Jesus as the Christ keeps us as the church faithful to the task of doing something constructive about the present crisis. To this end we ask for God's guidance and strength to be his obedient servants, with a love and respect for all of God's creation.

May the peace of God that passes all understanding keep our hearts and minds through Christ Jesus. Amen.

Sermon delivered on June 8, 1975
Resurrection Lutheran Church
Hamilton Square, New Jersey

Pentecost 5
Romans 8:18-23; Luke 6:36-42

Acceptance, Forgiveness, And Camping

> *Be merciful, just as your Father is merciful. Do not judge, and you will not be judged; do not condemn, and you will not be condemned. Forgive, and you will be forgiven; give, and it will be given to you ... Why do you see the speck in your neighbor's eye, but do not notice the log in your own eye? Or how can you say to your neighbor, "Friend, let me take out the speck in your eye," when you yourself do not see the log in your own eye? You hypocrite, first take the log out of your own eye, and then you will see clearly to take the speck out of your neighbor's eye.* — Luke 6:36-38, 41-42

Grace to you and peace from God our Father and the Lord Jesus Christ.

"Acceptance" and "Forgiveness" — two appropriate and typical topics for Sunday morning sermonizing. But because of the informality of a July weekend morning, let me try an untypical approach.

I would like to begin this morning's sermon with sort of a self-confession and reveal a particular negative attitude I had toward certain people.

During the Fourth of July week, my wife and I took a day off and went camping at a campsite just off the Appalachian Trail in High Point State Park near the New Jersey, Pennsylvania, and New York state borders. We went to hike the Appalachian Trail to get used to carrying heavy backpacks and get our legs and feet ready for our vacation in August, when we plan to do extensive hiking.

Another major reason for this July day of camping was to get away from the hustle and bustle of Route 33, and noisy teenage

59

backyard swim parties, and televised Watergate. In other words, we went for just a day to get away from it all and participate in the quiet and solitude of nature and listen only to the mysterious but quiet sounds of the forest night and perhaps the crackle of a campfire.

The camping area was very nice. It was for tents only, and each campsite was isolated from the next by fifty yards of forest. After about a six-hour hike and then a refreshing swim in a cool mountain lake, we returned to the campsite to enjoy the quiet of a beautiful, still July night. *Then it happened!*

Our neighbors in the next campsite through the woods moved in. They came in about two or three station wagons, and when they all got out of their vehicles, my wife and I were certain the circus had just come to town. It seemed as though there were about 25 children of various sizes and shapes yelling, screaming, and crying throughout the forest. They were followed by two or three barking dogs, one of which was a huge German shepherd that looked like a cross between a wolf and a grizzly bear, a creature who projected a never-ending bark that I am sure was heard and feared in nearby New York and Pennsylvania.

Following this parade were about four adults who seemed to enjoy yelling at each other and yelling at all the children and animals. One adult male had a knack of standing in the middle of the campsite screaming orders, peppered with obscenities, about the correct way to set up the tents, tables, chairs, and what sounded like four transistor radios.

One of the unique features of their finished camp set-up was that they had about six pressurized gas Coleman double-mantle lanterns, which I am sure together threw off more light than the surface of the sun. All in all, their nearby section of the forest, as evening fell, took on the appearance in both sound and sight of Times Square.

And so the night went. I had gone to the mountains for quiet, rest, and solitude, and instead, all night I listened to children crying, and the "top 50" rock and country songs on numerous radios. I listened to the high-pitched barking of little dogs, the deep resonant bark of the monster dog, the loud, cruel laugh or hostile yell of adults, and the constant pop-swish of opening beer cans.

In my sleeping bag, I almost hated those people. I was too much of a coward to go complain to them; I was certain they were incapable of reasoning with me and besides, I was afraid their dogs would rip me apart.

In my mind, as I lay awake in my sleeping bag, I tried to think of ways I could get those degenerates legally.

The next day, I came home to put the finishing touches on my sermon for last Sunday — a sermon specifically about women's liberation but ultimately about Jesus' message from Luke where he had welcomed and had eaten with the outcasts of his day.

I had already written for the sermon, "Each one of us, each one of our neighbors is important, immeasurably important. Each person is a free center of decision and responsibility, with a history and present capacity for fully developed, loving relationships with other people. We must respect and love each individual even though he may not be just like me or the way we would like him to be. Jesus offers us together forgiveness and the possibility for total life and joy in serving others."

Here I was, at least mentally, scheming how to get that loud-mouth family in the woods.

Looking back, I see I had been rationalizing. In the sleeping bag, I felt I did not fall into the sometimes-easy trap of hating their kind. (They were from Brooklyn.)

I certainly didn't hate everyone from Brooklyn. Everyone from Brooklyn or the city doesn't have to prove himself or herself to me. I like to think there is no prejudice in my mind. I honestly take each person as an individual and I had made individual judgment and decided that night in the tent. I was going to get that loud-mouthed individual family.

In last Sunday's Confession of Sins, I said, according to *Celebrate*, "I was slow in forgiving, too proud of myself; I said of many sins I am guilty, I ask you, my sisters and brothers, to forgive me and to assure me of the joy of the Lord."

And you answered, according to *Celebrate*, and I am sure honestly, "God forgives you, we forgive you."

And that meant much to me after that camping experience.

I had forgotten that at times you don't have to like someone to love them, to care for them and about them, to be concerned for their ultimate well-being.

God's plan for life is a communion where people dwell in a loving relationship with the creator of life and with one another. It should be a joint existence.

The family in the woods, through not only their general lifestyle or even their unbearable loudness, but through their yelling at one another, through their vocal bitterness toward the crying children, and through their lack of concern or respect for others around them — was living out of harmony with God's purpose for existence, as I was in my mental scheming, in my thoughts, words, and deeds of selfishness.

Today's gospel parable comes to mind.

> *Why do you look at the speck in your brother's eye, but pay no attention to the log in your own eye? How can you say to your brother, "Please, brother, let me take that speck out of your eye," yet not even see the log in your own eye? You hypocrite!*
> — Luke 6:41-42 (paraphrased)

We are selfish, sinful creatures. I could not help them that night; but knowing I am as they can be and are, in God's forgiveness, I receive the strength to strive to bring together others and myself in forgiveness and acceptance and respect and love. We do exist in and for one another; it is being a part of true life.

At this point, I would like to comment on some mixed thoughts about "sin" and "grace," which are really at the heart of any discussion of forgiveness and acceptance, and in so doing, let us try to penetrate the deeper levels of our life.

Sin does not mean an immoral act, and sin should not be used in the plural. We should not talk about "sinners" and "non-sinners." Sin is rather the great all-pervading problem of our whole life.

Sin is separation — separation from other people, separation from yourself, separation from the ground of meaning, and a self-imposed separation from God's intention for existence.

It is self-destructive, but we all equally participate in it. We are estranged from something to which we really belong and with which we should be united and our whole personality is involved.

"Grace" on the other hand, is the knowledge of the unity of life, a sensing and revelation of the way things should be.

Grace is the acceptance of that which is rejected. Grace is the reunion of life with life. Even in our knowledge of and state of sin, grace occurs in spite of separation and estrangement.

It is reconciliation of the self with the self. It changes guilt into confidence and courage, and our life as Christians is a struggle between this separation and reunion.

Jesus revealed the way it should be, but our selfishness constantly pulls us apart.

Often in a very refined way, we seek the pleasure of self-elevation. We put ourselves above loud campers from Brooklyn, we enjoy seeing the high-paid, cocky, big guns in government knocked down.

When people in the world and country and county starve emotionally, mentally, and physically, and injustices abound for others including family and friends, it seems quite often that thoughts and actions turn to number one, to ourselves.

In both humankind and nature, life is separated from life. This is the way we are, and this includes the most sensitive of humans. Man is split within himself. Life moves against itself through aggression, prejudice, hate, and despair.

It is a mixture of selfishness and self-hate. We are not capable of merciful, divine love toward ourselves or others. And when we abuse others, there is the abuse of ourselves.

The state of our whole life is estrangement from others and ourselves. We are separated from the mystery, the depth, and the greatness of our existence. We know the way it should be; we hope for that.

From today's epistle, Paul wrote,

... not just creation alone, but we who have the Spirit as the first of God's gifts, we also groan within ourselves as we wait for God to make us his sons and set our whole being free. — Romans 8:23 (paraphrased)

But now we are separated and yet bound, estranged and yet belonging, destroyed and yet preserved.

It was here that Christ revealed God. He revealed that in the midst of your separation, you are totally accepted, and when the understanding of this grace strikes you, you can then accept yourself and you can be reconciled to others. You are accepted!

It brings meaning to empty lives that are in despair because of having violated other lives when we know we should have loved.

God's acceptance can give meaning right when our indifference, our weakness, our hostility, and our lack of direction and composure have become intolerable to us.

It can come to us when we are fed-up with the apparent facts that things just don't seem to change and when despair destroys all joy and courage.

You are accepted by the power of life and existence, not for anything you did but because you are life.

In that moment, grace conquers sin, and reconciliation bridges the gulf of estrangement. Nothing is demanded of this experience, no religious or moral or intellectual presupposition — nothing but acceptance.

In the light of this acceptance, in the light of this grace, we perceive the power of grace in our relation to others and to ourselves. It is reunion of life with life. It breaks separation.

We experience the grace of being able to accept the life of another, even if it is hostile and harmful to us, for through grace, we know that it belongs to the same intention to which we belong and by which we have been accepted.

We can then love life, love others, and love ourselves, not because of our goodness and self-complacency, but because of our certainty of the eternal meaning of our life.

I would like to close this morning's sermon with a prayer that deals outwardly with praying hands but inwardly deals with our topic of forgiveness and acceptance in our hearts and personalities. Let us pray.

These hands that grip steering wheels and flick light switches, turn doorknobs, press typewriter keys, push brooms, lift dish towels and fold laundry, guide pencils, hold children, wield heavy tools, fine instruments, and intricate machines.

These hands I fold — a symbol of restraint of my own activities so that I might concentrate on what I am saying when I pray, "Into Your hands I commend myself."

Your hands, once tiny, holding your mother's little finger or fumbling with a toy; those hands that rested on the shoulders of burdened people, that passed out food to throngs, that lifted little children high, that touched the eyes of men and made them really see; those hands that touched fevered brows with cooling relief, that drew saddened people near; that restored total life.

Those hands broke bread and passed the cup.

Those hands You surrendered to hammer and nails and death.

Those hands revealing scars were raised to communicate to men God's peace, forgiveness, acceptance, and love.

Those hands stretched out to us beckon and invite — and so we come to hands far stronger than our own, at your hands to receive strength for our own weary, failing hands — strength to draw away from greedy grasping and selfish seizing.

Take these folded hands.

Open them to receive your love and to share that love with others whose hands have long been cold and empty and far too often crushed and crippled by selfish and thoughtless people.

You have made us members of Your body, forgiving our stiff and unbending paralysis.

Strengthen us to be the hands that reach out in your name to the lonely, the frustrated, the frightened, the exhausted, the bitter, and the hopeless with your love, with your acceptance, so that hands everywhere may be raised in praise to you, whose hand is ever upon us to hold us fast and to give us peace.[1]

May the peace of God, which passes all understanding keep our hearts and minds through Christ Jesus. Amen.

Sermon delivered July 15, 1973
Resurrection Lutheran Church
Hamilton Square, New Jersey

---

1. Karl E. Lutze, *Forgive our Forgettings, Lord!* (St. Louis: Concordia Publishing House, 1972), pp. 43 ff.

Zoom Lens

*King Herod heard of it, for Jesus' name had become
known. Some were saying, "John the baptizer has been
raised from the dead; and for this reason these powers
are at work in him." But others said, "It is Elijah."
And others said, "It is a prophet, like one of the prophets of old." But when Herod heard of it, he said, "John,
whom I beheaded, has been raised."*

*For Herod himself had sent men who arrested John,
bound him, and put him in prison on account of
Herodias, his brother Philip's wife, because Herod had
married her. For John had been telling Herod, "It is
not lawful for you to have your brother's wife." And
Herodias had a grudge against him, and wanted to kill
him. But she could not, for Herod feared John, knowing that he was a righteous and holy man, and he protected him. When he heard him, he was greatly per-
plexed; and yet he liked to listen to him. But an opportunity came when Herod on his birthday gave a ban-
quet for his courtiers and officers and for the leaders
of Galilee. When his daughter Herodias came in and
danced, she pleased Herod and his guests; and the king
said to the girl, "Ask me for whatever you wish, and I
will give it." And he solemnly swore to her, "Whatever
you ask me, I will give you, even half of my kingdom."
She went out and said to her mother, "What should I
ask for?" She replied, "The head of John the baptizer."
Immediately she rushed back to the king and requested,
"I want you to give me at once the head of John the
Baptist on a platter." The king was deeply grieved; yet
out of regard for his oaths and for the guests, he did not
want to refuse her. Immediately the king sent soldier of*

the guard with orders to bring John's head. He went
and beheaded him in the prison, brought his head on a
platter, and gave it to the girl. Then the girl gave it to
her mother. When his disciples heard about it, they came
and took his body, and laid it in a tomb.

— Mark 6:14-29

After her beguiling, hypnotic dance before the dinner guests, the young girl approached her uncle, Herod Antipas, who was now also her stepfather because he had abandoned his previous wife to marry the young dancer's mother; the girl ran to her stepfather with a request. "I want you to give me at once the head of John the Baptist on a platter." Her stepfather sent a soldier of the guard with orders to bring back John's head. The soldier rushed to the prison and cut off John's head, quickly returned with the severed head on a platter, and gave it to the girl.

We come to church on a pleasant, summer Sunday morning to hear the gospel, the good news, and what we seem to get with this morning's assigned text is *Nightmare on Elm Street* and *Natural Born Killers*, a gruesome R-rated-for-violence tale of lust, greed, misused power, and blood revenge. "I want his head on a platter, and I want it now." And Herod immediately fulfilled the young dancer's request.

What is going on here? How did this story slip into the biblical record, into holy scripture? This is the only narrative in the gospel of Mark that does not specifically mention Jesus or the disciples of Jesus. Why is this a gospel reading?

Actually, the story of John the Baptist is at the heart of Saint Mark's confession that Jesus is the Christ, that Jesus is God, present with us and for us, even in the midst of our sometimes violent, unjust world. John the Baptist — his message, his person, his death — is a crucial component in the book of Mark's confession of faith.

There is a fascinating children's picture book titled *Zoom*. With each turn of the page in this book, the reader takes a step back, in a sense, and has a better view of the subject portrayed in the book — a more inclusive view. As each page is turned, the reader is offered a more complete understanding of the subject. For example, on the first page of the book is a picture of what appears to be an aerial view of a Midwestern farm. Pictured on the page is a barn, a silo, and a grove of trees. It is obviously a farm.

But on the next page, as if looking through the lens of an imaginary video camera that is zooming away from the subject, frame by frame, we discover that the farm is only a toy farm set and we can see now, as our vantage point moves further back, a child playing with the small farm figures. Turn the page, and we discover that the child and toy farm are just a picture on a toy catalogue cover. What is the whole story? Turn the page and we can now see a boy holding the catalogue, and he is on a deck chair on a cruise ship, which, a page later turns out to be a poster on the side of a bus. It becomes as confusing as real life. We keep turning the pages to find out what is coming next, how all this will end, and where it is all going.

Astute young readers find clues on each page that provide a hint of what's coming next, but it's not until the last page, at the end of the book, the final picture, that we see the total context. Not until the last page is the truth revealed.

The same author/artist, in another book titled *Re-Zoom*, attempts to play with not only spatial relationships but also with time and culture. As you turn the pages in this book, ancient Egyptian people are revealed to be just hieroglyphics on an obelisk in the middle of a street in nineteenth-century Paris which, turn more pages, is actually part of a modern movie set, and so on and so on, until the end of the book where it is all made clear.

The gospel of Saint Mark is a *Zoom*-book with a surprise ending. And the part John the Baptist plays is of prime importance. As we turn the pages and work our way through the various symbols that form the story of John the Baptist, we are ushered through a multitude of different perspectives that guide us to the divine gift revealed on the last page of the gospel of Mark. John the Baptist prepares us, including offering clues on each of his pages, prepares us, in terms of space, culture, time, and meaning, to see and comprehend the big picture, on the last page.

Let's zoom in!

John the Baptist is where all four gospel books actually touch down in history together to begin the story of the ministry and message of Jesus, and foreshadow the final page of the story.

> *In the fifteenth year of the reign of Emperor Tiberius, when Pontius Pilate was governor of Judea, and Herod was ruler of Galilee ... the word of God came to John son of Zechariah in the wilderness.* — Luke 3:1-2

That is how Saint Luke affixed the message in real time.

The book of Saint Mark actually begins on the first page with John the Baptist, and it is that first picture that has set our mental image of John. From chapter 1:

> *John the baptizer appeared in the wilderness, proclaiming a baptism of repentance for the forgiveness of sins ... Now John was clothed with camel's hair, with a leather belt around his waist, and he ate locusts and wild honey.* — Mark 1:4, 6

John the Baptist.

My first mental image of John the Baptist was from Sunday school picture books. As I envisioned him, it was John as a "wild man," stomping out of the desert wilderness wide-eyed, insect-parts sticking to his mustache and bushy beard, his hands sticky from wild honey, matted hair in disarray, shouting words of fire and brimstone to Galilean villagers who were probably freaked out by John's appearance. I could envision frightened villagers nervously whispering to one another, "Who is this guy? Call 911. Get him to mental health."

But if we could zoom in on that time period, and when the four gospels were compiled and first circulated, John the Baptist was not viewed as a wild man, but just the opposite. Far from being considered in the gospel communities as a wide-eyed eccentric or some spaced-out hermit, John was actually viewed as a person that we should also aspire to be if we are to be faithful children of God in stressful, trying times. They believed that John knew the will and promise of God, and that even under very difficult circumstances — with all the pressures of a culture becoming more pluralistic, and the alien occupation of the Roman empire demanding compromises of one's traditional value system — the Jewish faithful believed that John was one person who remained faithful to God, and, according to the text, they flocked to him to be baptized. John was the image of faithfulness.

Turn the pages and look at all the pictures. According to scripture, John ate locusts and grasshoppers. At first glance today, that may seem awfully strange.

I remember when I was just a child, on one of our family sorties into Manhattan for the day, between museums we browsed through the exotic food section of some West Side deli, and my little brother, Tim, convinced my parents to purchase a small box of chocolate-covered grasshoppers. The deal was, we all had to eat some. They tasted like mini-Nestle Crunch bars.

Tim, who would become a biology major in college and later a bio-technician, broke them apart before eating them and identified the body parts: ("Hey look, here's a thorax and here's an antenna.") It was all very exotic and Bohemian. John the Baptist must have been pretty strange!

But turn the page. Soon after that first experience eating grasshoppers, I read in *National Geographic* or someplace, that grasshoppers or locusts (without the chocolate) are a very common food for those living on the edge of deserts; in fact, they are an excellent and readily available source of protein. And most importantly, according to Jewish guidelines at the time of John, locusts (along with wild honey) were listed as ritually "clean" foods. In other words, John was eating kosher, as well as healthy. What the pictures on the biblical pages show is that everything John did was faithful to the law of holy scripture.

And John's camel hair clothes? Along with wool and goat hair, camel hair is still the typical attire of desert Bedouins — durable and warm for the cold desert evenings of honest work.

Turn another page. Living in the wilderness was not viewed as antisocial or psychotic behavior. At the time, it was viewed as faithful behavior; the wilderness was considered uncontaminated by religious or political impurity.

The wilderness was also a place at that time of escape for those who rebelled against the local enforced rule of the Roman-Gentile occupation and its perceived idolatry. The wilderness was a place of retreat, exile, and hiding but also a location of no compromise to one's religious principles.

Turn another page. Perhaps of paramount importance, the wilderness was a symbol of religious hope — a place to receive insight into God and to receive God's guidance and blessing. The wilderness was the prime place for meditation and spiritual reflection, a place to be close to God.

Turn another page! See the wilderness as a "historic symbol." It was the location of escape and revelation for the chosen people of the exodus, the site of Mount Sinai and the divine gift of the Ten Commandments. The wilderness from which John emerged was considered the corridor to the promised land, to the promise of God. This is where John was coming from.

John was not something radically different. He was perceived as representing a return to the hope and promise of the Hebrew scriptures and ancient prophets; and people longed for direction in difficult, confusing times. As we turn all these pages of perspective and symbol, zooming along, where is it taking us? John emerged from the sacred wilderness to proclaim that one is coming who will be the corridor not to some new promised land elsewhere, but to God now present even here.

But the story of John reveals even more. What happens when our society is confronted by the way and will of God? The structures of human power including lust, fear, jealousy, and blood revenge are challenged by the prophetic word of a compassionate God. Human selfishness can lead prophets of God to a beheading or a crucifixion.

Today's gruesome narrative of the death of John, spokesperson of God, warns us of the risk of leading the prophetic life, which we are all called to do; and it foreshadows the arrest and execution of Jesus. But is this the last page of the story? Is this where it all ends, with Herod and Herodias sitting on the throne of final control?

The gospel authors considered John the Baptist to be the last, great prophet, speaking with the same authority as Isaiah. He emerged from the hope of the wilderness to bridge the old and the new divine promise to present life, and to set the stage for the coming of the Christ into this often unjust and brutal world, for the historical reality of Jesus.

We know now that Mark's story does not end with the death of John. We must keep turning the pages. Jesus moves into a life-altering ministry in Galilee. He then journeys to Jerusalem. And he, too, is executed by the human forces of greed and revenge. But it is only on the last page of the gospel of Mark that we can see the total picture; it is that last page that holds all of creation together, and that which blesses our sacred co-humanity. The final page is the victory of divine love over any injustice and even the reality of death.

John the Baptist sets us up for the good news. I should have mentioned earlier one other children's book of the same genre as *Zoom* and *Re-Zoom*, though by a different author. This other book is titled, *Looking Down*, and it reverses the process of the book, *Zoom*. *Looking Down* takes the reader on an excursion that starts in outer space. The first page holds a picture of the earth as a blue and white globe floating in the black of space.

But as you turn the pages, things become closer to home, and we can now see the mountains and the lakes, and then closer still to see towns and communities, until the book ends in a child's own backyard.

While *Zoom* starts with the very small and ends with a sense of the infinite, the book, *Looking Down*, opens with the extraterrestrial big picture and closes with the very familiar. God in flesh is also part of the message of the baptist's narrative. "I have baptized you with water; but Jesus will baptize you with the Holy Spirit" (Mark 1:8 paraphrased), is how John in Mark's gospel put it early on. Here is the Son of God in your own backyard, John proclaimed. This Christ is for you!

John the Baptist — *Zoom*-book for God. I believe that our contemporary culture in many ways mirrors the context of Saint

Mark's Greek Testament period — that mixing of often opposing or contrasting ideologies and powers and affiliations that occurred in Palestine at the time of the Roman occupation.

This age of John the Baptist was also like our present times, when many people were reaching out for some meaning, some sense of divine purpose. Today we are in great need of people who can assume the role of a contemporary John the Baptist, faithful people who can connect the old and the new and effectively point others to the reality of the living Christ, who can lead others to the last page of the sacred story.

It is, of course, risky. There will often be various forms of lust, greed, revenge, and the misuse of power and authority, who will want your head, and maybe on a platter. It is not easy to take a stand before the powers that be — for justice, for inclusive compassion, for effective peacemaking, for being Christlike.

> *John the baptizer appeared in the wilderness, proclaiming a baptism of repentance for the forgiveness of sins ... Now John was clothed with camel's hair, with a leather belt around his waist, and he ate locusts and wild honey.*   — Mark 1:4, 6

How can we take on that role today and bring others from the wilderness to the water — from death to life — from the first pages to the last page of the gospel story in the book of Mark, which is a picture of the empty tomb?

Sermon delivered July 13, 1997
First Lutheran Church
Duluth, Minnesota

Coney Island

> *He was praying in a certain place, and after he had*
> *finished, one of his disciples said to him, "Lord, teach*
> *us to pray, as John taught his disciples." He said to*
> *them, "When you pray, say: Father, hallowed be your*
> *name. Your kingdom come. Give us each day our daily*
> *bread. And forgive us our sins, for we ourselves forgive*
> *everyone indebted to us. And do not bring us to the*
> *time of trial."* — Luke 11:1-4

One of the disciples said to Jesus, "Lord, teach us to pray."

"Teach us to pray." That's a dangerous request. If one is serious about this, it is a risky thing to ask Jesus. It can be life-altering. "Lord, teach us to live! Teach us to align our priorities with your priorities." This is risky behavior.

Prayer is not just our turning to God, but it also involves an act of God — a divine act by which God draws us into the realm of inclusive love. In genuine prayer, you may actually become what you were meant to be from the very beginning, who you were intended to be by God. This is life-altering. It is a risky request, "Lord, teach us to pray."

Prayer is sometimes discovering the world's problems first in yourself. In prayer, you may actually enter into the neighbor's fear and pain. As the Lord's Prayer states, we pray not only to "my God" but "our Father." It is the God of us all that is addressed and answers. This is dangerous territory! What kind of world is this that we ask to enter?

If a child asks for a fish will you give her a poisonous
snake instead; if your child asks for nourishing food to
eat will you give him a scorpion?
— Luke 11:11-12 (paraphrased)

Too often we live in a world where we expect to give and receive poisonous snakes and scorpions — but that is not the way it
is to be with you who knows Abba, Father, God through Christ.
Prayer is perceiving the world in a whole new way. Prayer is letting God love the world through you.

"Lord, teach us to pray." This is a dangerous request, because
you shouldn't pray unless you are willing to become the answer.
Prayer is dialogue with the living God. It is being open, vulner-
able; it is deep confession; it is the readiness to be surprised by the
profound love of God, surprised by resurrection. "Thy kingdom
come, thy will be done" — do we really mean that?

"Lord Jesus, teach us to pray."

The first draft of this sermon began to sound like a lecture on
the nature of the healing, surprising, centering nature of prayer,
but it is summertime, and lectures are more wintry in nature. So
instead, I will tell you a summer story, a true story.

Lord, teach us to pray.

Our Father, holy is your name. Your kingdom come.
We want your will to be done. And forgive us our sins,
and may we forgive others.
— Luke 11:2-4 (paraphrased)

Sidney was playing the piano when I arrived at his apartment.
It was early summer — still June but hot and muggy and only
June. Sidney Pitts was the organist and choir director at the church
I once served in New Jersey almost twenty years ago. Our agenda
was to plan music for the summer worship services. It was hot and
muggy, and we were both tired of a long winter of meetings, and
our schedule was clear, so Sidney threw three or four nectarines in
a clear plastic bread bag. We got in his old Toyota Cressida and
drove up the Garden State Parkway and over the humpback Perth
Amboy Bridge to the turnpike and then over Outerbridge Crossing

to Staten Island and into the alien territory of New Yorkers. New Yorkers talk funny, and are often abrupt and rude; too often they are not "New Jersey Nice." It started to rain.

We drove past the Staten Island landfill with its infamous mountains of garbage being pushed about by bulldozers, disturbing the huge flock of resident herring gulls, who would then circle around and swoop down to fight over bits of trash. The smell of refuse in the humidity was overwhelming, as was the waste of resources represented there; all the greed buried in the now-poisoned earth by smoke-belching bulldozers. Even the gulls were corrupted, fighting over scraps of plastic that would eventually kill them. Our boastfulness, our desire to acquire, our alienation from the web of nature, from the good earth, what future does this hold? If your children want clean air and water and safe food, do you give them a scorpion? It appeared that way that day.

Like a giant cross on the skyline off to our right in the distance as seen from the height of the Verrazano-Narrows Bridge, was the rusted iron framework of the parachute-drop, and our destination, Coney Island.

It was a hot, June day and we really didn't want to plan summer worship services, and in one's freedom, sometimes, you just want to poke your head through the bubble wall of evil. So we went into alien territory. And also there was the pitiful truth that Sidney was a roller coaster addict. He had been patterned in youth by a careless father who loved dusty county fairs. Now Sidney's craving for speed and the fall was a serious addiction. He had flown on some of the great coasters of North America but never yet on the near-mythic "Cyclone" of Coney Island. I could only understand from a distance the inner, visceral, and mental demands of the severe addiction that was eating away at Sidney's soul. So I agreed that our weekly planning meeting that week could be held in Coney Island, with a slightly different agenda. You see, friendship often drags along accomplices even to places where people and things appear alien, radically different, and where the earth is so transformed by cement and garbage that one questions one's own origin and future. But that is precisely where the Cyclone lives — Coney Island.

We exited off the Belt Parkway and took West 17th Street straight toward Surf Avenue and the boardwalk. Tucked between Gravesend Bay and Coney Island, we should have traversed the lively birthing ground of a salt marsh. But there were no muskrats or snowy egrets, and no sweet sea and eel-grass smells. Rather, the pathway was graffiti-marked cement walls, abandoned storefronts, burned-out cars, blowing newspapers of yesterday's news in other places, crushed beer cans, rolling wine bottles, and an incredible amount of shattered glass shards, like mirrors reflecting the weak attempt of sunlight struggling through the clouds and urban haze. Even as one closed in on the sea, homeless men slept in doorways, and hairless, nervous dogs nosed throughout the gutter litter.

The empty boardwalk heading south was wide but worn. Nail heads rose a quarter inch above the splintered wood. Bike tires and bare feet, and I wondered what else, held no hope on this walkway.

Signs of past glory still littered the scene. There were large wooden columns painted to look like Italian marble though now you could see their pine grain heart. How much of our life together is just deception? We walked past the giant towering iron and steel structure of the parachute ride that had been moved here soon after the 1939-1940 World's Fair — a World's Fair just a decade away from the holocaust to come. The parachute ride stood, now a rusted remnant looking like the struts of an old wind-blown umbrella. Cables blew in the wind. Near its base was the cracked cement interwoven roadways of a kiddie car ride winding, weaving through four-foot weeds. It looked like something "after the bomb." Behind a fence were the carcasses of old "wild mouse" cars, their painted rodent faces and wide eyes streaked now with a veneer of soot and tears of splashed dry mud. A snarling German shepherd whose eyes seemed to remember caribou kills on Pleistocene tundra bared its teeth at us through a gap in a high wooden fence that was spray painted with the words, "White Power." What hope does even prayer have in such a place that we have made for ourselves?

As we walked north, ahead of us stood another fence and more weeds but behind them, and soaring above them, stood the smooth, clean lines of a fabulous roller coaster. Sidney's walk became a run. But as we approached the glorious wooden serpent, our expectation shifted into disappointment. The wooden support beams were streaked gray and split with age and darkened with moisture where they reached down to touch the sandy earth. Maybe that was the mistake: to come down from the heavens and touch this human world of decay. Does God now question the decision to send Jesus to us and to crucifixion? The rails were rusted, weeds dominating the lower runs. Its little train of cars sat before us, the rounded, low red image of speed, but now in a tight row, frozen, silent, impotent, the stuffing pushing out through cracks in the red leather seats.

It was the "Thunderbolt," the Cyclone's once-worthy but now apparently defeated competition. There were tears in Sidney's eyes. We were on Bowery, between 15th and 16th Streets. Our pilgrimage for amusement and meaning was becoming a nightmare.

We walked on and entered a part of the boardwalk that still offered some animation, though just barely. The giant Ferris wheel, the "Wonder Wheel," slowly, reluctantly, began to turn, lifting its massive caged seats in rotation with a groan. But it was empty. Newspaper pages blew by with their front page stories of drug-related murders, famine, and nations at war. An empty red, oval-shaped, fiberglass car crashed out of a pair of swinging doors. Above the exit door was the painted image of three or four screaming people in flames. Over the main gate to this "Fun House" (is that what this earth is — just a fun house — something for our pleasure — at the expense of others?) was a massive portrait of a devil, painted for cash by Soho artists in need of rent money; a devil and the words, "All ye who enter here: Abandon All Hope."

I looked out to where the waves were meeting the beach, the sea struggling to cleanse itself, and thought that there was no need to pay a dollar to ride an open car into the devil's mouth. One can walk there, even with a friend, and abandon all hope.

Finally, we reached our intended destination. Standing on firm-footed, newly painted, white support frames was the Cyclone — The Cyclone, towering and winding and higher than expectations. Sidney was breathing heavily. The coaster was waiting for customers — waiting for us. At last, things seemed right. The rest of the world may be in decay, hungry, homeless, and polluted, but we were going to get the thrill that we wanted, that we deserved!

The track arched its back eight times and the downside of the first arch was the wicked fall of fame. Infamous — from above and below on the first fall it appears as though the cars and lives plunge straight into the sand. And they do, as the tracks twist slightly south during the drop to give the added sensation that the cars have disengaged from the track. The hole at the foot of the first drop was added, according to tradition, when a competitor built a coaster slightly higher than the Cyclone. But the Cyclone would be second to none — only first. That's our desire after all, to go only "for the gold"; anything else is a loser.

They dug a hole and became number 1 again, with the added illusion for the rider of actually crashing into the earth, entering a sand tomb, being swallowed in a moment of darkness, before being yanked out and up again for another fall.

There was no waiting line when we bought tickets from a silent figure behind bars. And no line to get on the cars. As some of you know, for the full effect before you actually get in the car of a roller coaster, there should be a long line of nervous, bragging people, a fifteen minute wait at least. This is an important psychological trapping of the great old coasters that was denied us that afternoon. A long line giving you time to think about the destiny of chance, and our freedom of choice, and the thrill and threat of a technology that claims to be able to keep speeding cars on flimsy tracks pieced together by human hands and minds that may have been tired or angry or intoxicated or in pain when they nailed the framework together that will support our lives. "Father, forgive us...."

We walked too fast past the psychological props that were present — the white wooden signs with red lettering that lined the wall of the walkway to the waiting cars, signs that read,

- Heart Patients and Pregnant Women should Exit Immediately;
- Remove your eyeglasses;
- Remove pens and pencils from your pockets

- Remove wigs; and
- The Management is Not Responsible for your Injury or Death.

A metal "safety bar," which mocked its name, sort of a slippery chrome tube was snapped too loosely across my lap. You could easily be sucked out of that car in seconds, it seemed. And then the head-snapping start, the cog gear engaging, and the click-click-click-click-click as the little open train made its slow ascent up the old shaking timber frame. (I mean this was the real thing, not those slick steel and hydraulic coasters in new theme parks, and their promise to county commissioners to be fail-safe, and their computers pacing Swiss-made metal precision on rubber tires.) The Cyclone was the real thing. The foundation we shared shuddered and creaked and moaned ... "Even though you are young, you are mortal," it whispered. As we reached the very top, in that momentary pause, that for some of us seems like forever, before the fall, Sidney was in ecstasy and yelled out to the dark sky, "This is it! This is it!" For me it was a time of prayer, but in this prayer for safety, was I really open to God's complete answer?

The drop was as terrible as I had feared it would be.

As we stood by the exit gate, Sidney appeared to be sad. "It was a good ride," he said, "a fine coaster," but not the "ultimate thrill" that he longed for, not the ultimate fulfillment. "What could that be?" he said to himself, "to own a roller coaster? To be famous and ride a roller coaster? Maybe jumping off a roller coaster?" What would do it? What to hope for next? What to live for?

Well, Sidney stayed with the Cyclone. A purist must re-ride a coaster from different locations on the train, front, back, middle, for an objective evaluation. I walked a few blocks north along the boardwalk and past the boccie courts, to the New York City Aquarium. Beluga whales are more my speed, and if you walk to the roof and have patience, these small white whales with built-in smiles will come up to the top of their tank and complain to you about their confinement and squeak out their remembrances of the open sea.

81

Later that afternoon, Sidney and I walked back toward the car, back through this alien territory of Coney Island, when it began to happen. I believe God opened our eyes, answered prayer: "Thy kingdom come." People began to arrive, spilling with laughter from elevated trains that were spray-painted with Hispanic poetry of force and a certain dignity. It was a mixture of people from every race and place and experience, which could have been perceived as threatening and different, alien; driving us to even a deeper loneliness. Super urbanized and socially, emotionally, linguistically, and culturally different from Sidney and me and yet, at that moment, so much the same. What hope, if any, do they and I share — what future, what purpose? They celebrated life as they walked by me. They, too, smiled and laughed and teased and appreciated the ocean breeze. An old gray man limped past coming from the beach, with his pant legs wet and his feet sandy; he carried a full bucket of surf clams freshly dug at low tide, certainly more than he could ever eat alone. Not alone! These were clams to be diced for one of his favorite recipes from the old country. Tonight it was going to be, I am sure, chilled wine and white clam sauce for his linguine shared with a whole family; he had a big bucket full of clams. Let's invite the daughter's family over from Queens with all the kids and get a couple of loaves of garlic bread. It was to be a family celebration; you could just tell.

Heading toward the beach was a noisy group of interracial children, all wearing the same bright yellow T-shirt of some local day care center; they were smiling and kidding and holding hands that were ready to dig in the beach sand. Maybe, if their teachers were in a good mood, they would be allowed to get their feet a little wet after piling all their sneakers in a big red, white, and blue pile. They were so joyful together.

Hispanic teenagers glided by on the boards together to the sound of their oversized boom boxes, together on a clearing, "Welcome to summer" Friday afternoon. And the humidity finally seemed to lift as if the ceiling of things was raised and there was breathing room.

Food stands were now open for business around the Astroland Arcade, and they reflected clearly the parade of people, of us: Our past and positive pride; potato knish, kosher pizza, and southern barbecued ribs. "Real lamb" was promised on the blackened shish kebab. There were Spanish meat pies, moussaka, and fresh mussels in a Tabasco marinara sauce to be eaten in a celebration with friends who understand you and respect you.

The "All Beef" hot dogs at Nathan's were, to my taste at that awakened moment, excellent! My hot dog was handed to me by a young dark-skinned woman with Asian eyes who seemed to be a mix of all of us, and her smile was haunting. That concession counter was only a temporary stage in the process of her living, her being, and she knew that well.

We were a mixed and motley group but shared more than just an unconscious yet common desire to face death together on the Cyclone and re-emerge with our personhood intact.

We need forgiveness. I need forgiveness. "Father forgive us our sins, as we should forgive others."

We are the same community; we plunge into the sand together in this place, from wherever we come from — Brooklyn, Jamaica, Newark, the old country, St. Paul, or Duluth.

Jesus defended and lived our right to care, to affection, to acceptance, not to be abused or neglected but defended, including the good earth. He was called where we are to nurture, to respect, to protect the sacredness of all these others from any forces that tear body, mind, or soul asunder. For when minds and bodies and cities decay, a part of us all decays. Any attempt to marginalize or belittle or mistreat, any bigotry, any prejudice, any inflicted pain and suffering is an affront to us all, and to God called "Abba" Father, the loving parent of us all.

As Sidney and I walked back to the parking lot before a fast-approaching thunderstorm, once again we walked through the area of most disrepair and decay, back through the graveyard of past joy, through the weeds and rust, the area of the park we had thought was long and forever dead, where before there seemed to be a despair feared to be too thick for hope.

"Thy kingdom come, thy will be done."

We heard a rattling sound, and a click, click, click, click, and we saw the movement of open cars on the old wooden arches that

83

loomed ahead. Gifts of life were being offered even here. Even now. Once again. The old Thunderbolt roller coaster was alive. An old carny with a straw hat and cigar was beckoning us toward the red coaster cars, which were losing their stuffing but not their heart.

Other people appeared, laughing, sharing joy among themselves that spilled over to us, and together we entered and filled all the car seats, and, like a phoenix, we rose together above the ashes and rubble of decay and difference, transcending together both loneliness and chaos.

During that slow ascent, pinned to the back of our seat as the cars nosed toward the heavens, a teenage boy in the seat directly ahead turned his head with a laugh to look around at Sidney and me. We laughed back. Sisters and brothers in front and in back of us, in my history now and my future. They were a part of my responsibility now, and me of theirs; finally together in intended unity, glimpse of thy kingdom come; our final reunion with a loving, living, eternal God. As we reached the arched peak, there together we shared for a moment a view of an endless ocean. Above us and before us actual lightning bolts slashed the sky of Coney Island. There were grand claps of thunder. But no fear! And we fell together, yet, of course, rose again, united in the time-stopping and space-connecting speed of it all.

Sidney and I walked back to the car through the weeds and litter that bordered the parking lot, but it was all different now. What can we do about hatred, disharmony, and separation? We are called into servanthood in our world. Love centers unity and responsibility.

"Your kingdom come, your will be done, dear Father God."

We drove over the high arch of the Verrazano-Narrows Bridge heading for the Parkway, and north and south, and the beginning and the end, alpha and omega, seemed united. We were reunited....

"Lord, Jesus, teach us to pray." Amen.

Sermon originally delivered August 13, 1978
Resurrection Lutheran Church
Hamilton Square, New Jersey

Sermon revised and delivered July 26, 1998
First Lutheran Church
Duluth, Minnesota

Dealing With Our Fears

After this Jesus went to the other side of the Sea of Galilee, also called the Sea of Tiberias. A large crowd kept following him, because they saw the signs that he was doing for the sick. Jesus went up the mountain and sat down there with his disciples. Now the Passover, the festival of the Jews, was near. When he looked up and saw a large crowd coming toward him, Jesus said to Philip, "Where are we to buy bread for these people to eat?" He said this to test him, for he himself knew what he was going to do. Philip answered him, "Six months' wages would not buy enough bread for each of them to get a little." One of his disciples, Andrew, Simon Peter's brother, said to him, "There is a boy here who has five barley loaves and two fish. But what are they among so many people?" Jesus said, "Make the people sit down." Now there was a great deal of grass in the place; so they sat down, about five thousand in all. Then Jesus took the loaves, and when he had given thanks, he distributed them to those who were seated; so also the fish, as much as they wanted. When they were satisfied, he told his disciples, "Gather up the fragments left over, so that nothing may be lost." So they gathered them up, and from the fragments of the five barley loaves, left by those who had eaten, they filled twelve baskets. When the people saw the sign that he had done, they began to say, "This is indeed the prophet who is to come into the world."

When Jesus realized that they were about to come and take him by force to make him king, he withdrew again to the mountain by himself.

When evening came, his disciples went down to the sea, got into a boat, and started across the sea to Capernaum. It was now dark, and Jesus had not yet come to them. The sea became rough because a strong wind was blowing. When they had rowed about three or four miles, they saw Jesus walking on the sea and coming near the boat, and they were terrified. But he said to them, "It is I; do not be afraid." Then they wanted to take him into the boat, and immediately the boat reached the land toward which they were going.
— John 6:1-21

Evening came, and the disciples went down to the lake, got into a boat, and started across the water to Capernaum. It was dark; Jesus had not yet come to them. The water became turbulent. A strong wind was blowing. A stormy, watery chaos. They were deeply afraid.

The following conversation was actually overheard on a commercial airplane right before takeoff, immediately following the cabin steward's standard, required safety speech about personal belongings safely stored in overhead storage bins or under the seat in front of you; and words about seat belts, cabin pressure, and descending oxygen masks. A father and his five-year old son clicked on their seat belts, and the little boy who had listened very carefully to the whole flight safety speech, asked his father, "Dad, why do we need floating seat-cushions?"

The dad said, "Just in case they're needed."

The son said, "Is it in case the wing catches on fire, and we have to land in the water?"

Dad responded, "Well, I suppose that's the right idea."

The son replied, "Okay." But a few moments later he said, "Dad."

"Yes, son?"

"Dad, you know I'm scared of lobsters."

There is a lot to fear in our life together, and we all have our inner fears, but I believe that there are some things in life that are more worthy of our fear than others. What is it that can ultimately harm us or others? The disciples were in the water, in the dark, and a storm arose. Where was Jesus? They were terrified.

The montage of stories and confessions that forms our holy scripture speaks of all kinds of fear. The biblical word knows well the various emotions and phobias of the human mind and soul. Our scripture certainly speaks of the primal fears of fire, flood, and famine, the misty unknown of the twilight dissipating into the dark of the night, or the searing intrusion of a lightning bolt, the roaring lion, and the hooded snake of the ancient Mideast. There are fears generated by objects and phenomena known and unknown: a drought, bandits, sickness, an enemy, all of which may generate fear but a fear that can also, in fact or theory, be conquered by action, by changing the situation, or removing the source of the fear. The Bible, in fact, implores us to work together to help to remove, if possible, the source of fear from ourselves and from others: feed the hungry, heal the sick, comfort those in distress, live in peace. God does not desire us to live in fear or pain.

However, the Bible also takes us much deeper into our intended humanity, and therefore, it speaks most precisely and profoundly about a different kind of fear, a different quality of anxiety. It is our fear of being worthless — of being or becoming nothing — of living with no lasting purpose — of ending with no meaning. It is a fear of being abandoned with no final unity with those we love.

It is a fear that can become manifest at any and every moment, even in situations where there are no objects to be feared. Fear of fire or heights or a hooded snake may be a part of our individual psychological makeup. Psychotherapy may help to remove these as fears in our experience, but that other fear, deep within all of us, is ontological: fear of being abandoned by all, totally separated. It is embedded in our sacred humanness. And in the face of this, it is only the true word of God, spoken perhaps through friend or foe or stranger or symbol, or by an angelic messenger, by an inner faith; by the living Christ; it is only the living word of God that can say to us with any grounded authority, "Be not afraid! Fear not, for I am with you. Fear not."

*When evening came, his disciples went down to the sea
and started across to Capernaum. It was dark. Jesus
had not yet come to them. And a storm arose, a great
storm, and they were terrified.*

                — John 6:16-19 (paraphrased)

We have actually two marvelous, connected stories in today's
assigned gospel text: The feeding of the 5,000 and Jesus stilling
the storm.

Does this sound familiar? People on a grassy hillside overlooking a large lake, wanting to hear the good news, the gospel
spoken? Boats on the lake, and I bet you are hungry, also. What a
great setting, this morning in the park, to hear these stories![1]

Much of the good news of God held in these texts is well known
and loved by many of us — the feeding of the 5,000 — Jesus healing, teaching, and feeding those who were hungry, feeding all their
needs, body, mind, and soul, offering them what they need to be
whole. We know that wonderful section in John's text when some
followers of Jesus who say it can't be done, what with limited resources; all we have is a few loaves of bread and a few fish. Yet
with God's help, people were fed, and our blessing can be shared.
This is, after all, the bread of life we are talking about.

Jesus walks on the water to still the storm without and within,
to bring peace. We know these stories well, but as you get to know
me, you will discover that I want to go beyond the obvious or well-
worn, to look with you at some of the often-overlooked signs and
symbols of the word of God in the text. Today it involves a glance
at our inner fears, those that can justifiably terrify us.

Let's look closer at the scripture. Our reading states that Jesus
went to the other side of the Sea of Galilee, also called the Sea of
Tiberias. That is named after Tiberias Caesar, who claimed to be
God. Maybe the inclusion of this name for the lake was an attempt
for it to be more recognizable to non-Jews as the gospel story spread
out in the Mediterranean world. There is more implied here. In
Jesus' lifetime, the city of Tiberias was just being built on the west
bank of the Sea of Galilee. It was built on top of an old Jewish
cemetery. It was at the time of Jesus and the early church, a symbol

of the arrogance and paganism of Rome. Caesar could build any-
where he wanted, even on holy ground. Caesar could even change
the name of the lake from Galilee to Tiberias. Faithful Jews refused to enter this new city of Caesar's for it was unclean. But
Tiberias soon became the place where the money and power was
located. Some local people soon compromised their beliefs and
traditions and went to Tiberias to wheel and deal with the pagan
Romans. All this tension — hate and fear of Rome — entered the
story of the feeding of the 5,000 for many who first heard it, when
the name Tiberias was included in the text.

The text adds that the Passover, the festival of the Jews, was
near. For those who knew the true story, thoughts would race ahead
to Jerusalem and soon a last supper, a betrayal, a horrible death.
That last supper also appears with these words: "Jesus took the
loaves, and when he had given thanks, he distributed them to those
before him." The people respond, "This is indeed the prophet who
is come into the world." They would have Moses in mind, who
also did signs and wonders and went up a mountain, like Jesus in
today's text, to confront and listen to God. However, is Jesus just
another Moses, Moses who lies buried in an unmarked grave, or is
this Jesus something different, something more?

Jesus then goes by himself up a mountain, which is the traditional place to be open to God. He goes up alone, like Moses, and
seems to be gone, separated from his disciples. Gone from us. In
the exodus story, that was when they fashioned a golden calf.

The disciples go down to the water and enter a boat and start
across the sea to Capernaum. This detail of location, to Capernaum,
is also unique to the book of John; the other texts that tell this story
seem to have them heading the other direction, south toward Jerusalem. But the book of John has them heading back toward
Capernaum. Capernaum was their home base. This was where Jesus
and they had lived together during this part of his ministry. They
were attempting to go home, when a great storm arose.

We should remember that at the time of Jesus, a night storm on
the water was not just rough sailing. It was a sharp, unsettling reminder of chaos. A night storm on the sea would drive one back to

the opening of the book of Genesis before God separated the waters and created the sun and stars and formed dry land. Before God created order, there was only swirling water in endless night. This was that storm on the sea, back to chaos, before God brought harmony, peace, and meaning. The disciples thought they were alone in the chaos. Where was God? Where was Jesus? Not with them they assumed, but away somewhere, high in the sky on some mountaintop. They were alone on the sea, separated, and they were deeply afraid; they were terrified.

If we are ultimately alone in this life, separated, we have good reason to fear; the deep fear is of being abandoned by God.

Listen to the good news: Even in the darkest moment of their despair, there was Jesus, walking through the storm, over the churning waters of chaos. "It is I. Be not afraid," said Jesus according to the text (John 6:20 paraphrase).

Those words, "It is I," can be accurately translated as "I am."

"I am who I am. Be not afraid." It is the voice of the burning bush in the wilderness heard by Moses. It is the very presence of God. "It is I. Don't be afraid" (reference to Exodus 3:14 and John 6:20 paraphrase).

Suddenly we are projected to the very end of the gospel story. Remember that morning. The disciples, followers of Jesus, women and men, were walking/running out of the dark night, through the early morning mist, and into the cemetery. They were running through the city of the dead, past the entrances to tombs, marked and unmarked, some now neatly camouflaged by time, crumbling, and blending into the surrounding limestone cliffs and hills.

Some tombs freshly dug and carved out were obvious intrusions into the rock and earth of time and place, containers making so obvious our finitude. And according to scripture, when the women came to their destination of human death, they stood anxious and full of fear. An angel spoke pure truth, the same words: "Be not afraid."

And Jesus spoke: "Why are you weeping? Why are you looking among the dead for one who is alive? I am — Fear not!" (reference to John 20:13 and Matthew 28:5 paraphrase).

When evening came, his disciples went down to the sea, got into a boat, and started across the sea to Capernaum.   — John 6:16-17

When my father, who is a Lutheran pastor, retired, he gave to me as a gift some of his old books. They included the 1942 edition of *The Journals of Henry Melchior Muhlenberg*. It was a wonderful gift, though I must admit that I have not read all of it yet. It contains several volumes and totals about 3,000 pages.

I find the journal fascinating not only because of its glimpses of life during the early stages of the European colonization of Eastern North America, but also because Pastor Muhlenberg was such an amazingly faithful person. From his home base in eastern Pennsylvania, he traveled between 1742 and 1787 preaching in German, Dutch, and English from Nova Scotia to Georgia, organizing Lutheran congregations along the way and striving for unity in the midst of some rather wild and woolly diversity.

He and his wife had three children — three sons. One became a pastor and a major-general in the Revolution who wintered with his good friend, George Washington, in Valley Forge. Another son became a botanist who gave the Latin names to many North American trees and other plants. He became president of Benjamin Franklin College, which later merged to become Franklin and Marshall. The third son was the first speaker of the Continental Congress in the new United States.

On my birthday, I became curious about how Father Muhlenberg had celebrated his birthday over 200 years ago. Did his famous sons and their families come home for a big birthday bash? I randomly picked out a year and looked up his journal entry on his birthday. Well, on that day Muhlenberg had made absolutely no mention of his birthday. He was traveling near Manhattan Island. This was his birthday journal entry:

I departed from Flushing in a small boat. The wind was contrary and a storm arose and we had to pass through some dangerous areas where many ships had floundered. The ship's company consisted of three Quaker women and three sailors. The wind was so violent that

93

it seemed the ship would turn over. When I saw the danger and that help was needed, I sprang to the aid of the sailors, but I was quicker with my hands than with my feet and I slipped over to the lower side of the ship which was riding under water, and would have fallen overboard if I had not caught hold of a fastened sail and pulled myself out of the water. It was a rough passage, and the Quaker women kept shouting and crying for help whenever the ship ... threatened to turn over. I told them that they ought not to scream and act like heathens if, as they professed, they really had an inborn light and inner spirit ... it would be much safer to learn and believe and live according to God's revealed Word; then, in time of danger and death, the Holy Spirit would bring it to their remembrance and comfort them. The storm abated and we reached New York safely.[2]

Muhlenberg had an Easter faith not tied to lily bulbs and butterflies or benevolent Mother Nature or some contrived concept of "good death." Rather, he was grasped by the revealed and loving-living Word of God, the God-force of creation and all eternity, God incarnate — Jesus walking over the troubled waters to us.

It was God-I am — God who affirms our call for justice; who infuses grace into worship; who can offer genuine forgiveness; who enables reconciliation and resurrection; and who bursts through social, racial, cultural, religious bigotry, and idolatry. It is God who points to the equality of all his daughters and sons, and to the loving interconnectedness of all existence. God is present and available even in the chaos of the inner storm. We are free, no longer terrified by lobsters or abandonment. We are free to serve.

"When evening came, his disciples went down to the sea, got into a boat, and started across the sea to Capernaum" (John 6:16-17), where they had lived with Jesus; they wanted to go home. But it became dark; Jesus had not yet come to them. And the sea became rough because a strong wind was blowing, and they were terrified. But then they looked out and saw Jesus even there, walking over the troubled waters. He spoke to them, "I am. It is I. Do not be afraid." They took him into the boat to be with them, and the text states, "immediately the boat reached the land toward which they were going" (John 6:21), Capernaum. With Jesus, immediately, they were safely home.

Sermon delivered July 27, 1997
First Lutheran Church
Duluth, Minnesota

---

1. This reference is to Leif Erikson Park, which contains an amphitheater and is across from the church where this sermon was delivered. Summer worship services (July and August) are held there, at the shoreline of Lake Superior.

2. Henry Melchior Muhlenberg, *The Journals of Henry Melchior Muhlenberg* (Philadelphia: Evangelical Lutheran Ministerium of Pennsylvania, 1942-1958).

Bread Of Life

*Do not spend your whole life working for, striving for,
dreaming about food that will perish, but strive for the
food, the nourishment that endures eternally, which
Christ offers to you.* — John 6:27 (paraphrase)

*Jesus said to them by the lake, "I am the bread of life. I
am. Whoever comes to me will never be hungry, and
whoever believes in me will never be thirsty."*
— John 6:35 (paraphrase)

I had bread on the mind this whole week as I was studying this
gospel text and preparing for this sermon. I kept thinking about
bread. I like bread that has substance — bread that has internal and
external integrity. I say this not in a flippant, careless way, but I
love bread. Sometimes I dream about bread. Bread can so natu-
rally combine both the ordinary and extraordinary.

Let me tell you about some bread that I have tasted, such as the
warm, thick-crusted, round rye bread from Macy's Cellar in Manhattan. Take a number from the deli counter, and get in a long line
of people representing about every racial, cultural arrangement that
is imaginable and then some — a montage of people together, amazingly patient, talking to each other although strangers, joyful and
all waiting for marvelous rye bread.

There are some wonderful oval, black pumpernickel loaves in
a little bakery owned and operated by an elderly couple in Yorktown
that test the strength and condition of your teeth, yet are always
well worth the workout. And the bakers, flour on their aprons and
cheeks, greet you with a smile as they offer you their artwork.

There is sourdough bread bought off small, outdoor, wooden carts on the docks in Seattle and eaten on a crowded pier with smoked salmon or a slice of pepper-jack cheese. The sound of the harbor is a part of the meal, and everyone seems to be in such a holiday mood, together on the pier — a surprise party centered by sourdough bread.

I remember those extraordinary, slender two-and-a-half-foot long, eight-ounce French baguettes that are carried home with the newspaper after work or sticking out from bicycle baskets throughout the narrow streets of old French hamlets, long thin bread that has a shelf life of only a few hours, but with crackling crisp, golden skin and elastic, creamy interiors, alive with the flavor of fresh-milled wheat. I haven't been to Paris in years, but I keep handy a map of the downtown that marks the locations of the ten bakeries that make the best baguettes in the city as judged by the Paris edition of the *International Herald Tribune*. One never knows when one may be forced to make a quick trip to Paris, and I just want to be prepared.

I won't even talk about croissants; they are much too sensual for a family-friendly Sunday morning worship service.

In India, in remote, back-country temple towns, there is a crisp, flat bread that is encrusted with hot pepper spices, and served with steamy, sweet tea. In the heat of the pre-monsoon season, you can sit in the shade of a tree, tear off pieces of the bread, and with newfound friends talk about each others' families and faith.

I remember waking up early, after sleeping on a couch at a friend's brownstone on New York's West Side in the early autumn, putting on a sweater and walking over to one of the 24-hour bagel shops around 82nd Street and Columbus Avenue. They are not upscale bagel and cappuccino cafes with outdoor tables and steep prices but small shops that are mostly ovens and wicker baskets overflowing with bagels. Carrying back the bagel bag still radiating oven-captured heat within — bagels chewy and crunchy crusted (cream cheese and lox secondary or unnecessary), provided a fresh bagel breakfast with old friends where we talked together about our hopes and fears for the future. This is one of those moments when it is all right to be off-guard, when one is accepted and loved, a guest in the home of a gracious host who serves newly born, warm bagels.

I once bought some fry-bread from three Navajo women who had set up a propane, portable stove in a park in Cortez, Colorado, on a windy day in July — fry bread with honey. The women carefully watched us and silently hoped we liked the bread. It was a grandmother's recipe. We must have told them ten times that it was wonderful bread. And they knew, I believe, that we really meant it, and for a moment our two cultures came together over bread in a city park on a windy summer day many years ago. I wished I could have shared my grandmother's breakfast breads with them.

When we were living in or visiting family in New Jersey on our wedding anniversary, Shirley and I would often go to a restaurant in an old gabled house near the beach along the Rumpson River, just up the street from Bruce Springsteen's house in Fairhaven. It was a restaurant run by a Swiss couple who has bread flown in from France fresh each day, which seems rather excessive and wasteful until you taste the bread. It is bread worthy of blessing our wedding anniversary and wonderful marriage.

I once walked from the ancient springs that form the source of the Jordan River, high in the hills near the Golan Heights and the Syrian border. I walked toward Galilee through the green band of trees that hug the small, lazy river. Today it is a disputed border area known in Israel for its hostile diversity — Arab, Jew, Palestinian, Druze. There are signs warning of minefields so I stayed on the path, and I came upon an old stone mill built soon after the time of the Crusades. There was a man and a woman there, Palestinians, grinding wheat with an ancient water-powered millstone. And there was also in the dark corner a blazing oven. The woman was baking large, thin flat bread. She offered me bread and yogurt. According to the scriptural record, Jesus had walked this same path, and the bread he ate along the way with his disciples would have looked and tasted like the bread I ate at that moment with a Palestinian couple with whom, all of a sudden, I felt a kindred closeness.

I have this wonderful recipe for hard rolls. It is a long, arduous process of letting the dough rise and punching it down, letting it rise and punching it down, forming rolls and painting them with egg white, then finally ending the process by placing them right out of the oven in a cold draft to get that crackly glaze. My recipe makes about a dozen rolls and the problem is that as soon as they come out of the oven, Shirley and I, with butter ready, eat them all. In less compulsive, more compassionate moments, we catch ourselves and call the children or call over some neighbors. The rolls are too good not to share.

I remember one Thanksgiving dinner, a family gathering in Hershey, Pennsylvania. I was perhaps in high school at the time. The meal was a magic time to laugh, to remember, and to consume large amounts of food all shared around a large oval table. Toward the end of the meal, Great Aunt Verna went back into the kitchen to bring out the dessert pies and discovered that we had forgotten to bring her homemade rolls to the table. This would have broken the tradition of the family holiday circle. So, though filled with turkey and rabbit and dumplings and multiple expressions of potato, we said, "Bring on the rolls." They were bread but more than bread, so fresh and alive and lovingly prepared and shared. "Bring on those rolls."

At the time of Jesus, the Nabatians carved passageways and rooms into the steep, red-rock cliffs in a wilderness area on the caravan route in present-day Jordan. Today, Bedouin descendants of the Nabatians still inhabit some of these cave dwellings, and if you are climbing around in those mountains and are lucky, Nabatian families will invite you to share small bread cakes and hot tea. We could not speak the same language, but we could play with the children and share the bread. In the Bedouin culture, if you share bread you are, for that moment, a part of their family, to be protected and respected along with being fed, "one family" as you share the bread.

Let me say it again: Shirley and I were once in a forest outside of Saint Petersburg, which was then called Leningrad. It was the height of the Cold War. We were standing in the snow, in a pine forest, on New Year's Eve. We were with Russians who had had very little contact with anyone from the United States. And we had had very little contact with real-life, living, breathing Russians. It was very cold and dark in the forest outside of Leningrad in late December. But then, out of the forest (this was the reason we were all there, it was a New Year's Eve tradition) came the Snow Queen, a young woman dressed in white fur. She was bringing in the New Year with gifts for us all. She carried a large serving dish, and on the dish were the traditional gifts of hope. On the plate were salt and a large, beautiful, braided loaf of bread.

We all then quickly went inside by a fire and shared the bread and some four-star cognac; and for all of us, at last, the cold war was over.

Do you sense the universality of this bread sharing?

Before moving here, friends and colleagues wished us safe travels and asked why we decided to come to Duluth and First Lutheran Church? So I told them about this congregation — the profound sense of Christian community and mission and the talented, engaging members — a job description that seems to match my vision of ministry. So why did I really come here? On my second visit during the call process, in the midst of a full, even grueling day of interviews — the members of the call committee and Shirley and I paused together for a meal in the upper commons, and in addition to some very tasty stew, there was, served in baskets, some incredible bread — wonderful bread — multiple varieties of braided, glazed, beautiful, aesthetically pleasing, chewy, heavenly bread, passed around the table with a conversation of good humor and Christian insight and mission, including a concern about justice and feeding those hungry due to famine or war. So why did I really come to Duluth? There is some beautiful bread here — very fresh and alive and lovingly prepared and shared.

Sometimes God seems so theoretical, so conceptual, such a remote concept; but when we are together sharing bread and drinking the fruit of the vine under the umbrella of the empty cross, God seems very real and personal and present. God with us in the sharing of bread and the remembrance of past meals and in the hope for a loving future together. All of us — those who have sown, tended, reaped, gathered, milled, kneaded, baked, transported, marketed our daily bread; farmers, sailors, bakers, truckers, merchants — there is a desire in the breaking and eating of bread to bless them all, and hope that they, too, know the peace and love of God.

I am talking about bread of substance that you can touch, smell, bite into, feel good about, and share with others. Bread that you know is a grand gift that we don't really deserve but is offered to us, and then eaten in joyful community. You always want more of that bread, and you just know instinctively is good for you. Bread that you dream about — that is physical yet gives a hint of final harmony, and that is the bread of life — God.

> *Jesus said to them, "I am the bread of life. Whoever comes to me will never be hungry, and whoever believes in me will never be thirsty."*   — John 6:35

> *Jesus said, "Take and eat; this is my body given for you. Take and drink this is my blood, shed for you and for all people."*   — Matthew 26:26-28 (paraphrased)

Sermon delivered August 3, 1997
First Lutheran Church
Duluth, Minnesota

Namibia

*Now when Jesus came into the district of Caesarea
Philippi, he asked his disciples, "Who do people say
that I am?" They responded, "Some say you are John
the Baptist, but others say you are Elijah, and still others say Jeremiah or one of the other prophets." Then
Jesus said to them, "But who do you say that I am?"*
— Matthew 16:13-15 (paraphrased)

In the past year or so, I have had a number of opportunities to
preach on this story that is recorded in Matthew and Mark and
Luke — the story of Jesus' conversation with his disciples as they
walked into the region of Caesarea Philippi. The last opportunity I
had to preach on this text was just six Sundays ago in Namibia, in
southwest Africa. I preached the sermon in a very interesting congregation in the capital city of Windhoek. It is a congregation that
is attempting something rather new in Africa. Some would call it
radical, maybe dangerous. I would say they are being reforma-
tional and faithful to the gospel.

The church was filled the day I preached, maybe 400 worshipers, and certainly not because I was there. Normally the worshipers spill out the door and into the churchyard. The congregation is
perhaps 98% black Namibians, which may appear to someone from
the outside to be rather homogeneous, but it is not. It is a very
diverse group of people representing a variety of Namibian tribal
groups: the worshipers represented the Ovambo peoples, the
Kavango peoples, the Hereros, the Samara, the Nama and Sans
people, young and old. There were also a few white Germans, an
Indian from the Punjab, and a black woman from Uganda. There
were also a variety of educational backgrounds represented; and

103

worshipers who were financially poor and some who were economically well-off by Namibian standards. There were new Christians in the mix and those who were born into a long tradition of the Christian faith.

The diversity went deeper. The members represented three different church bodies that historically did not relate to each other very well because of the different ways they had responded to apartheid in the past. There was even a bishop of one of the church bodies in attendance the Sunday that I preached. It was a new community of diverse searchers in a new nation-state who shared a profound Christian hope.

In many ways, I found that congregation to be much like this worshiping community in Weaver Chapel at Wittenberg University. Most of you are members of various congregations in your hometowns located across the state and across the globe. You represent a mix of different denominations, certainly a variety of different traditions and worship styles. You are used to your own pastors and choirs and their music preferences. Some of you are not members of any church. There is a good chance you don't, at least this Sunday, know all the names of the people sitting in your own row. This gathering is a bit different from your pre-Wittenberg experience. In many ways we have come together like that Namibian congregation. We have formed a new community in an environment new to many of us. Is there a hope we share?

Jesus and the friends and students who were traveling with him entered into the region of Caesarea Philippi. They, too, were no longer in the familiar landscape of their past. Caesarea Philippi was not a Galilean, Jewish village with barking dogs to greet you, with the morning vegetable and bread stalls, friends gathered by the well for conversation, fishermen and women, farmers and shepherds, all the neighbors sharing the same cultural, tribal, and religious heritage. Caesarea Philippi was something very different. It was a new location and mind-set. Caesarea was named after Tiberius Caesar who claimed to be God; and Philippi after the Tetrarch Phillip, a son of Herod, who some would say sold his religious and spiritual heritage, his soul, for power. The disciples were entering a new world with Jesus.

The nation of Namibia is only six years old, since it gained its independence from South Africa in 1990. It had been through much pain and suffering. For well over a century, racial prejudice resulted in everything from resettlement to "ethic cleansing," including an extermination policy crafted by some of the same German officials who formulated Nazi Germany's policies of extermination. Early in this century, it was the official law of the European colonists to shoot on sight any members of the Herero tribe, for example. One year there were well over 100,000 Hereros living in their traditional tribal lands in central Namibia; three years later, about 80,000 of them were dead. The world did not complain, and a similar policy was enacted thirty years later by some of the same people in Germany — the holocaust. More recent sorrows in Namibia under apartheid involved a brutal war, families torn asunder, refugees flooding over borders, plus the destruction of land and property. The scars of all this are still very apparent; but it is now a new free, democratic nation. It seems to me that their capacity for forgiveness is enormous; and their unified concern for the vast numbers of poor in their nation is genuine.

The congregation in which I preached six weeks ago held many of the leaders of this new country — a developing nation entering our world of new technology, new models for economic growth; all the promises of the good life through the accumulation of material goods. But what gives substance to a hopeful future? What is there to strive for that has lasting meaning?

Jesus asked, "Who do the people in this new world of ours say that I am?"

I began my sermon in that Namibian congregation by reading a prayer that we often prayed here in worship at Wittenberg before Namibia's freedom in 1990, a prayer for our brothers and sisters in "occupied" Namibia asking God to protect and strengthen them and their congregations; a prayer that remembered their refugees in Angola and Zambia; and that called for the end of apartheid and all the human suffering that it causes. It was a prayer that we at Wittenberg prayed often, and a prayer that the Namibians, of course, not only prayed but lived.

Then I asked that African congregation, "It is now 1996. What prayer concerns should we offer together now, our worship community at Wittenberg University and you, our brothers and sisters in Namibia?"

I believe that we are facing together, in many ways, the same challenges today. That congregation and this congregation have a lot in common. As sisters and brothers in Christ in Namibia and here at Wittenberg, we need each other's support and prayers and insights as we all face together God's call to be faithful in a new global, pluralistic, postmodern world of opportunity and of great need and suffering.

Caesarea Philippi at the time of Jesus was an exclusive Roman government, a resort town in the mountains on a terrace overlooking the fertile north end of the Jordan River valley. It was a beautiful, water-rich, green, park-like location, like our campus. Passing the disciples and Jesus as they walked on the paved Roman road to Caesarea Philippi would have been the regional leaders of commerce and the military who were summoned to power-lunches along manicured gardens. Pre-dating the Romans, the place was still considered by many at the time of Jesus to be the home of the god Pan, the god of new wine and good times, the party god who calls you to seek your own pleasure, even at the expense of others.

Caesarea Philippi was quite a place, where the powerbrokers of the New Age came together to relax and cool down above the super-heated, summer plains of Palestine to do a little business with the Roman overlords; a location where those with big ideas came to sell their hopes; a place where the highly educated came to learn more; a place where people from all over the Roman world, with various religious and philosophical traditions, came together to strategize. It was a lot like Windhoek, Namibia, and Wittenberg University today.

In Caesarea Philippi there were multiple life philosophies and life expressions, some in harmony with each other, and some in wild disharmony; some worshiping the wealth and power and authority of Caesar, and many following the party-hardy Pan calling to you to forget your worries and your responsibilities to care for others.

It was precisely there in the territory of Caesarea Philippi (or was it Capetown or Columbus or our campus?), a setting perhaps where one is most free to see the clarity of choice. There, before friends and strangers and fellow searchers, in the midst of new possibilities for both blessings and despair, while in the background Pan played his flute of seduction. In this very setting, Jesus asked us to look carefully around us.

"Who do people say that I am?"

"Well," his disciples answered in all honesty, "some say you are John the Baptist," calling them home to past answers and promises.

"And others say you are Elijah or Jeremiah," knife-sharp prophetic voices from the past, and we do seek meaning and direction in these changing times that seem to lack satisfying inspiration, that lack a "moral compass."

Others say that they are rather comfortable with their present definitions of right and wrong; very comfortable; they are certain of their salvation. And you, Jesus, you just complicate things when you welcome the tax collectors, treat women as equals, accept the outcasts, and when you tell us to love our enemies. Some say you are too demanding; we want a religion that is more comfortable than what you offer.

Others listen very selectively to what you say, picking and choosing what best suits them, and what meets their perceived needs and their own prejudices.

You are going to run into students on this campus who will say that you, Jesus, are just one voice among many voices that reveal God; no big deal. One of the many possibilities leading to personal fulfillment — maybe all right; maybe all wrong.

Others say Jesus, you are well-meaning but naive. I mean, look at the realities of Caesar's money and authority. That's what I want; that's what I am preparing for; that's what I live for. I want to be respected for my accumulations, my good taste.

In Namibia, some say you represent an angry God who seeks blood revenge, death to our enemies.

"Who do they say I am?"

The common learning seminar this semester will be examining expressions of the "creative human spirit." One of the lives that you will examine in detail is that of Sigmund Freud who answered, "Jesus, I hope you are more than God because God is just an internal, psychological crutch formed by the human mind to ease the pain of living before death; nothing more. God is not a reality in the realm of physical existence."

"Who do people say that I am?"

Some say in the comfort of these new times, "It doesn't matter who you are Jesus, and it won't matter until maybe, at some later date, when I want to become serious about such things as commitment, religion, and worship again. In the meantime, Caesar rules the territory during the day and Pan with his cool, sweet wine rules the night."

Then, according to the text, it all became very personal. Jesus looked directly at those following him, those around him in this region of Caesarea Philippi, that congregation in Windhoek, Namibia, to us in the chapel, this morning, and Jesus asked, "But what about you? Who do you say that I am?" No room for hedging now.

This is not only the turning point in the book of Matthew, but for the Christian, it is the center of our life. Simon Peter replied, "You are the Christ." You are the one transparent to the source of a personal love that will never be finished!

"Who do you say that I am?" The Namibian congregation where I preached six weeks ago seemed to me to clearly choose a unity of purpose based on a confession of Christ; they wanted more than just a gathering together of diverse people, but they desired to worship and serve God as revealed by Jesus.

God is present in each new moment willing to make us whole, and desiring our actions to bring harmony and peace to everyone we encounter. Jesus, you are the Christ, the Messiah, God who affirms our call for justice; who infuses grace into worship; God who can offer genuine forgiveness; who enables reconciliation and resurrection; and who bursts through social, racial, tribal, cultural, religious bigotry, and idolatry. It is God who points to the equality of all his daughters and sons, and to the interconnectedness of all existence including the very earth itself. It is God speaking through the lives and actions recorded in holy scripture, and hopefully in our own personal diaries and dorm discussions.

Shouldn't this be the purpose of our gathering together here in Weaver Chapel in this new academic year, the reason why we come together for worship and fellowship?

It is all held nicely in Saint Peter's answer to Jesus. Through you, Jesus, God's unencumbered love flows unrestricted to us; and the unity of that divine love knows no boundaries, not time or space, not cultures or tribes or race or sex or age, not even death.

Jesus asked his followers, "Who do people say that I am?"

In this present new age of ours shaped by instant communication, new freedoms, old fears, HIV/AIDS, the continuing cry for justice, in classes tomorrow morning, they say, believe, and disbelieve all kinds of things about you, Jesus. Some say that you are a myth. Some consider you a principle of values that can be bought and sold. Some say that the God about which you speak is an idealistic wish, not reality. Many just don't know what to answer to such a question; they really haven't thought too much about it.

Then, according to our holy scripture, Jesus looks at each of us, and asks the centering question, "But what about you? Who do you say that I am?"

It is an answer that can shape one's future in ways of unity, blessing, and peace, and an answer to share with others.

Saint Peter responded to Jesus, and in that answer is what unites us with our sisters and brothers in that church in Windhoek and with the body of Christ around the globe, and it holds what should be the center of our ministry together this year at Wittenberg. It is the source of the hope, the peace, the direction, and the growth we seek in this new setting in Weaver Chapel, together in this new academic year.

Peter responded, "You are the Christ, the living God." Amen.

Sermon delivered August 25, 1996
Weaver Chapel
Wittenberg University
Springfield, Ohio

Forgiveness

*Then Peter came and said to him, "Lord, if another
member of the church sins against me, how often should
I forgive? As many as seven times?" Jesus said to him,
"Not seven times, but, I tell you, seventy-seven times."*
— Matthew 18:21-22

I am going to begin this sermon with its conclusion; I am going to start with the ending: Where there is forgiveness, there is life. When you forgive you are a part of the eternity of God's love.

Luther put it this way in the *Small Catechism,* "Where there is forgiveness of sins, there is also life and salvation."

*For the sake of your Son, Jesus Christ, have mercy on
us. Forgive us, renew us, and lead us, so that we may
delight in your will and walk in your ways, to the glory
of your holy name.*[1]

*Peter came to Jesus and asked, "Lord, when my brother
or sister wrongs me, how often should I forgive? As
many as seven times?"*
— Matthew 18:21 (paraphrased)

If you think about it, that was a rather generous offer by Peter, to forgive someone seven times. To say from the heart, "I forgive you," and then, "I forgive you, again. Yes, from the depth of my being, in mind and soul I really do forgive you this third time." And to do that seven times! It certainly goes beyond the normal, everyday expectations of the workplace. If someone wrongs you again and again and again, and you forgive from the heart seven times, that is very generous.

But that's not what Jesus said. Jesus (as the Christ, as the voice of God) replied, "No, not seven times but seventy-seven times" (Matthew 18:22 paraphrased).

Our culture is somewhat comfortable with relatively large numbers. We may drive a car hundreds of miles at a time and buy items that cost thousands of dollars. Such numbers actually mean something to us. But there was an odd-acting quasar in the news last week. In the constellation Serpens, this quasar is about eight billion light-years away from earth. Let me think about that: eight billion light-years. If light travels at the speed of 186,282 miles per second, in a year it will cover about six trillion miles (that is a six followed by twelve zeros). Six trillion miles; now I must multiply that by eight billion to determine how far away this quasar is from me. For most of us, there is a point where certain numbers cause our eyes to glaze over and the mind to fog up; they stretch beyond comprehension.

There is some question over the translation of the Aramaic of the text. Does the word Jesus used mean "seventy times seven" or more likely "seventy-seven"? It really doesn't matter. On the street in ancient Palestine, pre-calculator, almost pre-science, that seventy-seven figure was practically incomprehensible. An accurate translation of Jesus' response to the question of how many times should we forgive would be "forever. Forgive forever!"

Just in case someone misses the radical nature of that answer, Jesus tells a radical parable. Jesus presents his audience with a drama in three acts.

Act I: The reign of God may be said to be like a ruler who decided to settle accounts with the servants. Jesus sets this story in a hypothetical location, some eastern empire where there were non-Jewish customs and laws, where, for example, one could sell a spouse and children to pay a debt which was not allowed in Palestine at the time of Jesus. I believe Jesus set the story in a vague, abstract location so those hearing him would not be distracted by thoughts of a specific ruler or region and miss the inclusive word of the parable.

Once upon a time, there was a ruler, and a servant of the ruler owed an incredible amount of money. In Greek, it says that the servant owed the ruler 10,000 talents. About the time of Jesus, all the revenue of King Herod from his total kingdom in one year was about 900 talents. The servant in the story owed 10,000 talents. A talent was the largest unit of currency in use at the time of Jesus, and 10,000 was the highest number used in counting. In other words, this character owed the ruler billions and trillions of dollars! The sale of one's property, family, and one's very self wouldn't come close to paying off even a fraction of what was owed. It was hopeless. It was utterly hopeless.

The servant asked the ruler for mercy and promised to pay back all the money owed if he would be given "a little more time," which would have been a real laugh for those first hearing the story. That was an impossible promise to keep. The servant knew it; certainly the ruler knew it. It could never be paid off.

However, Jesus said the ruler, strictly out of loving mercy, out of pure grace, forgave the servant and cancelled the debt completely.

There were no special deals and no interest payments; the ruler forgave the debt completely.

Now Act II of the play: Someone, a peer of the one forgiven, owes him 100 denarii, a small amount of money that could be easily acquired and repaid, which is what this person promised to do, using ironically, the exact same words of promise that were said earlier in the play by the ruler's debtor. But the forgiven one, unmindful of the forgiveness received, acts totally opposite from the ruler, and rejects the offer, grabs the debtor by the throat, and throws him into jail.

Then, Act III: The ruler sends for the ungrateful servant and says, "I forgave you! Don't you know the nature of forgiveness? Should you not have dealt mercifully with your fellow servant, as I dealt with you?" The ungrateful servant was sentenced to jail, literally in the Greek, taken to the "torturers" until what was owned would be paid back.

Then the important postscript to the story: Jesus said this parable is a story about God, who is like a loving parent, who forgives far beyond the pleas and even the understanding of the beloved children. It is about God who forgives way beyond the worth of anyone's human achievements. God forgives simply out of divine goodness and love, out of grace.

The result of accepted forgiveness is to be whole, to have a clear view of what harmony can be in human relations. I really believe if a person cannot forgive, it is self-destructive. In withholding forgiveness, not allowing it to flow through you, you are certainly less than what God wants you to be. Not forgiving is like turning yourself in for torture.

Such forgiveness is a radical concept, though certainly not an isolated scriptural event; rather, it is woven throughout the entire fabric of the Bible, from Joseph in our first reading this morning, forgiving his selfish, vengeful brothers, to Jesus on the cross: "Father forgive them, for they know not what they do." But it is so difficult for us, so difficult for me.

One time, at the college where I served as pastor, we sponsored a lecture and forum on the topic of rape. A guest speaker told about a personal experience. She was raped by her father many years before. She told her story with intense emotion and cutting rage — a deep inner anger. She said she would never forgive her father; she would always hate him and always wish suffering for him.

After her talk, I asked her about forgiveness — not forgetting and certainly still working to make sure this does not happen to others. We talked about working to make sure that others will feel free to speak about such horrible experiences and deal with what has happened to them. I could understand if she never liked her father again — okay. However, could she ever forgive in the sense of letting go of the hate, and even wish some healing for her father in his distorted state?

Well, she jumped all over me, saying something like I was another male who doesn't take rape seriously. I think the inner rage gave power to her message and her personal story, which brought an important message to places like a college campus, but the lack of forgiveness was eating her alive; it was so obvious, so self-destructive, and not just when she gave her lecture; the rape was still occurring.

114

Forgiveness frees the forgiver from being overwhelmed and devoured by the past. I believe forgiveness is a reality that is at the very core of what it means to be a Christian, at the very center of the gospel message. Often when we wish to share the message of Christianity, share the gospel, share the good news, or when we want to define God, we talk about love. We say, "God is love" or "We should love one another," which is okay if we go on to define what love means, and if we remember that the secular world has defined love in many ways, some of which can easily distort the essence of Christianity. Perhaps our primary strategy of evangelism should be to summarize the essence of Christianity, the good news, as a living word about forgiveness.

"But Lord, how many times do I have to forgive? Seven times?"

I have heard it put this way: "Without forgiveness of sins, there is really no future for us." When we have a serious falling out with someone and there is not forgiveness, our future with that someone is forever closed. The past then controls the future.

We have heard the pain in the voices of our brothers and sisters: "I hate that person. I know this is eating me alive, but I just can't seem to let it go. I know that I should pray about it and forgive even if I can't forget. But I can't pray; I can't even focus on anything but my hurt and my anger. I'm all knotted up inside, and I don't know what to do."

How can we offer good news? Maybe say something like, "Right now you probably cannot forgive him or her; it's too soon, the pain is too raw. But what you can or cannot do right now is not perhaps a particularly good gauge of what you maybe able to do in time, with a lot of grace."

Forgiveness is the way God has chosen to relate to a creation that has evolved into self-awareness and often chooses in our freedom the destructiveness of selfishness.

Forgiveness is a determination to seek the new; to be a peacemaker in a warring world; to refuse to give in to the corrosive cynicism of a consumer culture; to be light and salt; to be hopeful when despair drags people down; to side with the oppressed, the outsiders, the lost; to find ways to feed the hungry, clothe the naked, heal the sick.

115

A true story comes to mind: After retiring as a nurse, Janet Colby decided to work part-time as a school bus driver transporting elementary school kids. One day as the kids got off the bus at school, she didn't see Jonathan. She knew Jonathan had gotten on the bus, but now where was he? She walked to the very back of the bus, and there was Jonathan still sitting in his seat. His book bag was open and he was holding a jar of blue paint, which was also open, and there was blue paint all over his hands, all over the front of his shirt and his pants, and on the bus seat. Blue paint was at that very moment dripping onto the floor. Janet looked at him and said, "Jonathan."

Jonathan quickly replied, "I didn't do it," which seems to me to be the most common response of our society today. "I didn't do it."

I read about a stream that was polluted by chemicals that caused a massive fish kill. The toxins are traced directly to a pipe leading to a local chemical plant. How did the plant executives first respond? "We didn't do it."

Jonathan looked like he was going to be sick, but he said, "I didn't do it."

The next day, Jonathan stepped on the bus with a present for the driver. It was a drawing that he had made. Jonathan had attempted to draw a school bus with a stick figure of a little boy and a little stick figure of Janet Colby, the bus driver, whose big round head in the drawing contained a wide smile. A big balloon coming from the mouth of the little boy held these words, "I'm s-o-r-e."

Janet asked the young artist, "Jonathan, what does s-o-r-e spell?"

He said, "Sorry. I'm sorry."

And Mrs. Colby did smile and hugged Jonathan, who then also smiled.

When one knows that they are in need of forgiveness, they are not only sorry, but also sore; they are hurting. It hurts knowing something is very wrong and needs to be set right.

We must be responsible for our actions, and there are certain consequences that must be dealt with in terms of justice and preventing further pain. Forgiveness is not excusing unjust behavior.

Nor is it necessarily forgetting what happened. I am talking about forgiving, accepting that person as a fellow, sacred traveler in our life together, a child of God. Sometimes it is very difficult. In that forgiveness, there is, I believe, a glimpse of resurrection already now — a wholeness. It is the smile on the face of Jonathan and Mrs. Colby after the blue paint episode, when being sore turns to sorry and then turns to loving community.

A number of years ago, in St. Peter's Square in Rome, a young Turkish terrorist shot Pope John Paul. When the Pope, who was seriously injured, recovered, he went to the prison to visit his would-be assassin. In the bare, whitewashed prison cell, John Paul tenderly held the hand that had held the gun and had pulled the trigger. And the Pope forgave the young man. When the Pope emerged from the cell, he said,

> *What we talked about will have to remain a secret between him and me, [but] I spoke to him as a brother whom I have pardoned — the Lord gave us the grace to meet as brothers, because all the events of our lives must confirm that God is our Father and all of us are God's children in Jesus Christ, and thus if we are all God's children in Jesus Christ, we are all brothers [and sisters].*

The pope forgave the gunman, but the gunman remained in prison. We are still responsible for what we have done, accountable even with forgiveness.

Love takes the form of forgiveness and justice at the same time. And as I have said, we should not forget, for example, the horror and continuing impact of slavery in the United States or the European holocaust, or being abused in one's youth or in one's marriage. Not to forget, or revise the realities of such evil. And we should certainly take precautions so such actions of pain and separation will never happen again to ourselves or to others, along with perhaps steps now to rectify past injustices. But to become whole, as sisters and brothers, we must be open to the healing of forgiveness and to the hope for reconciliation. This is at the heart of the radical nature of Christianity, the revelation of God through Jesus.

Forgiveness frees the forgiver from being overwhelmed and devoured by the past. The forgiver is removed from the nightmare of revenge of prejudice or despair. "Father forgive them," even from the cross, is the Christ-model of the human living out the image of God. It is entering into God's point of view.

"Lord, how often should I forgive? As many as seven times?"

Whenever there is forgiveness, there is life. When you forgive, you are a part of the eternity of God's love. Amen.

Sermon delivered September 12, 1999
First Lutheran Church
Duluth, Minnesota

---

1. *Lutheran Book of Worship* (Minneapolis: Augsburg Publishing House, 1978), p. 56.

About The Author

Born and raised at the Jersey Shore, Michael David Wuchter earned his undergraduate degree at Wittenberg University in Springfield, Ohio, then returned to the East for his Master of Divinity degree from the Lutheran Theological Seminary in Philadelphia, Pennsylvania, and his Doctorate of Ministry Degree from Princeton Theological Seminary. He became a third-generation Lutheran pastor. Wittenberg University honored him for meritorious service in 1983 and he was a Fulbright Scholar in India in the summer of 1984.

Michael Wuchter served Resurrection Lutheran Church in Hamilton Square, New Jersey, from 1972-1979. Wittenberg University, where both he and his wife, Shirley, had been students, called him to become the Pastor to the University in 1979. He served eighteen years as campus pastor before moving back to a parish setting in Duluth, Minnesota. Three years later, while on a mission trip to a companion congregation in Oniipa, Namibia, Africa, his life ended unexpectedly at age 54 on August 5, 2000.

Shirley resides in Duluth. The Wuchters' son, Andrew, and his wife, Traci, also live in Minnesota. The Wuchters' daughter, Kirsten, her husband, Bob, and their daughters, Eleanor Grace and Hannah Ruth, live in Montana.

Printed in the United States
149371LV00002B/1/P

9 780788 026034